IN
SEARCH
OF THE
KINGDOM

OBEYA MICHAEL OBEYA

Order this book online at www.trafford.com
or email orders@trafford.com

Most Trafford titles are also available at major online book retailers.

Print information available on the last page.

ISBN: 978-1-6987-0310-7 (sc)
ISBN: 978-1-6987-0311-4 (e)

Trafford rev. 09/03/2020

 www.trafford.com
North America & international
toll-free: 844-688-6899 (USA & Canada)
fax: 812 355 4082

CONTENTS

LIST OF FIGURES

DEDICATION

I dedicate this book to my Lord and Savior, Jesus Christ, who saved me and leads me on my journey:

- I thank my father, Ignatius, for setting an example for me of a disciplined life.
- I appreciate my mother, Angelina, who nurtured and encouraged me.
- I appreciate my siblings Lawrence, Patrick, Linda, and the Late Robert, for being there for me whenever I needed them.
- This book is for my children, Mike, Michelle, Ene, and Idoko, as a guidebook for their growth.
- I thank my friends, Kay Logan and Elizabeth Wiley, who assisted me with preparing this book.

I am truly grateful for your support and encouragement.

Obeya Michael Obeya

PREFACE

The next few pages are a short synopsis of my person, background, and the development of my life. I have decided to share some of my personal stories to help the reader obtain a better perspective of the man behind the book (see Figure 1).

Figure 1 – The Author before the Pyramids During his Research Tour for this Book

I was born in Lagos, Nigeria, in 1965 to Ignatius and Angelina Obeya (see Figure 2). My father was an Army Captain. My mother was a flight attendant and a former schoolteacher. I became a Christian sometime around 1991 when I received the gospel of Jesus Christ and came to believe in God through him. I worked in the Financial Services business for many years, with some of the most successful firms in that industry. I left the Corporate world in 2008 to begin my own company in the United States as well as to give more attendance to my first love, the gospel of Jesus Christ. My business has provided jobs for many people to the glory of God. I studied scripture and eschatology during this time, and I hope to share much of what I have come to learn with you. I want to share the gospel's simplicity worldwide and demonstrate God's interest in our lives. I believe that I have been privileged from birth to associate with people that have influenced the world in one way or another. I intend to use the time God has given me to inspire them and others to follow the way of Christ in all that they do. I will now tell you a little bit about my early years.

My father was from the Northern region of Nigeria, while my mother was from the South East. My father was the first commissioned military officer from the Idoma ethnic group of Nigeria (today's Benue state). When I was two weeks old, the Nigerian military sent him to study in the United States Army School of Infantry at Fort Benning, Georgia. We were living in the United States when the first military Coup d'état in Nigeria occurred, resulting in the killing of the Prime Minister and other top government functionaries. Officers of the South East region were the primary instigators of the first Coup. Six months later, there was a counter-coup carried out by officers of Northern descent (my father's region).

Figure 2 – Author's Beloved Mother Some Years Before her Death

The social crisis that erupted because of these events is called the Nigerian Crisis of 1966. It began earnestly in July 1966 and continued for many months. It resulted in the murder of several innocent people of Eastern descent, primarily Igbos, who lived in the northern region. The reason for this was that the Northern citizens viewed the first Coup as a sinister plot by the Easterners to seize government by force. The counter-coup resulted in a stalemate of power between the South East region and the Northern region. A third region called the South West maintained neutrality.

After several conferences and meetings in different World and African capitals, the two sides engaged in the "Biafran Civil War." Biafra being the name the South Eastern secessionists named their new country. My father and uncles fought on the side of the Federal forces in this devastating war (Figure 3 has a picture of the leaders of both armies). In contrast, my uncles (from my mother's family) fought as Biafran soldiers. My baptismal godfather was the second President of Biafra. A man named General Phillip Effiong. I lost relatives on both sides.

Figure 3 – Former Biafran Secessionist Leader Ojukwu and the Leader of the Federal Forces, President Gowon Reconciled in Their Later Years'

As a child, I would look through pictures of some of those relatives and family friends of ours that had died on both sides and wondered how things would be if they were still alive. The senselessness of war and anarchy had an impact on my early life. Nevertheless, I had a happy childhood (see Figure 4). I drank richly from my exposure to all manner of cultures, both within and outside Nigeria. At six years old, I moved to India with my parents again and saw poverty for the first time in my life (see Figure 5). In those days, it was rare to see poor people in Nigeria. So, my sighting of poor people in India frightened me. I always wanted to reach out to the hungry-looking children I saw by the roadside and give them my school food. Later in life, I would see that same poverty in Nigeria.

Figure 4 – Author as a Toddler with his Father in Zaria
Just Before the Start of the Nigerian Civil War

A few years later, in July of 1975, the same northern officers who had fought together against the Easterners, participated in a Coup d'état led by a General named Murtala Mohammed. His Coup would rupture a subtle fissure that existed between the northerners who practiced the Christian Religion, and those who practiced the Muslim Faith.

However, General Murtala Mohammed had substantial support from the northern Christian officers to remove the Head of State at that time, a man named Jack Gowon, a Northern Christian. However, junior Northern Christian officers led a bloody counter-coup in February of 1976 against Murtala, resulting in his assassination. Northern senior Christian officers led by the Army Chief, a man named

Figure 5 – Author as a Child in his Mother's Garden in India

Theophilus Danjuma, squashed the Coup. He commanded a force headed by Colonel Babangida, who later became a military leader of Nigeria, to route the anti-government faction led by Colonel Dimka. Danjuma was my father's friend and coursemate as young military cadets (see Figure 6). With the death of Murtala, the Northern officers asked Danjuma to take over as Head of State, but he declined the offer. He supported Murtala's deputy to become Head of State, following protocol, even though he was from the South-Western part of Nigeria. The name of this man was Olusegun Obasanjo, the husband of my mother's elder sister, Evelyn. Obasanjo would go on to become not only a military Head of State but also one of the iconic leaders in Africa. During his first Presidency, my father became Nigeria's military Defense Adviser to Great Britain. I finished my elementary school in London and moved to boarding school in East Sussex, England. I enjoyed my time there, especially the sports and debating clubs for students (see Figure 7).

Figure 6 – Author's Father General Obeya in the Middle Front Row and General Danjuma, his Course Mate is to his Left

Obasanjo was elected much later as a civilian President of Nigeria, but not before serving a few years in prison for an alleged plot to overthrow a subsequent military government. During his years in prison, I managed the feeding contract of the penal institution where he was held and visited and prayed with him often. During our first meeting, I recall him excitedly calling out to everyone proclaiming, "this is my son; this is my son." I spent many days with him sharing the gospel. I recall one day when he looked at me and declared me a "Radical." He said this jovially because of my puritanical views on the Christian faith. Years after he would be released from prison and become Head of State again, I would try to speak with him about the conditions of the ordinary people in Nigeria. However, by this time, I had moved to the United States of America to further my education. It was difficult to synchronize a time to meet. I hoped to urge him to use his new faith to rebuild his country.

Figure 7 – Author in the Middle in the Top Row as
Captain of his High School Cricket Team

The experience of Obasanjo, falling from grace as a former head of state to the place of a prisoner and God's ability to raise him from that position to make him President again, is a profound testimony for what God can do in the lives of men, families, and nations. I sincerely desire for all people, most especially my people in Benue, Nigeria, to look back at my testimony concerning Obasanjo and know if God can do it for him, God can do it for us. The people of Benue must seek to walk in the righteousness of God, in every aspect of our lives, and commit ourselves to hard work and innovation. If we do this, we will roll away the stone for Jesus to raise us up as he once raised Lazarus.

I gave my life to Christ just a few years before Obasanjo's incarceration. I was, as I am now, anxious to reach everyone with the good news concerning Jesus Christ. I always had a "God sense" in me from a young age, but I never had the peace of God until I gave my life to Christ. I want you to know that same peace and that is why I wrote this book. The rest of the book will be less about me and more about Christ. I encourage you to read this book to the end and to know that I wrote it in love.

I shared these intimate portraits of my personal life to help the reader place me appropriately when trying to understand my writings and belief in Jesus Christ. I want you to see that every life has a purpose. No matter what condition you were born into, or are experiencing now; God has a beautiful plan for your life. All you need to do is to believe and trust in his Son Jesus Christ, and he will guide you to his predetermined destination. No matter how great or powerful you might be, live in humility with others because you do not know what is written for you tomorrow. The experience of my life from childhood had made me more sensitive to the diversity of people. I understand that no matter the differences between people on the surface, we are fundamentally all God's children. He wants us to enter a relationship with him in the person of Jesus Christ. As you go into this book, you will understand more about Christ through the work he has done in and through my life. I hope you are blessed and uplifted by my insight into Christ and God. By the end of this book, you will learn much about the more profound mysteries of God, and his message encoded within creation to help lead us out of despair and into his marvelous light. Remember, all things are possible to them who believe.

FOR THE KINGDOM OF GOD IS WITHIN YOU

YOU MIGHT BE HINDU, JUDAIC, A MUSLIM, A ZOROASTRIAN, A Catholic, an Ifa adherent, an Atheist, or any other faith. Nevertheless, the voice of the Son of God can be heard deep within your heart. I hope that after reading this book, you will realize that there is a living **man** named Jesus Christ. He watches over you and cares for everything that concerns you (both spiritually and physically). Even though you might not have received Jesus Christ into your life, the Light of Christ still speaks within you (Jn. 1:5).

The concept that Almighty God revealed himself in the person of a Man is a radically audacious one. God became man, is a concept that could only come from the mind of God himself. Who else would have the audacity to preach that and expect people to believe it? Little wonder men have tried to turn themselves and their leaders into gods.

This book is going to be different from most books you might have read on faith and its congruity with the development of man's rational Consciousness. It contains a lot of reasoning as well as truth apprehended through faith. The intent is to show that even within the realm of reason, the gospel of Jesus is a most logically sound message.

We analyze the condition of humanity, society, economies, natural sciences, and spirituality. It culminates in our decision about Christ as revealed in the Man Jesus Christ, the head of the Body of Christ. *"Therefore let all Israel know with certainty that God has made this Jesus, whom you crucified, both Lord and Christ"* (Acts 2:36). To obtain the most benefit from this book, you must study it to the very end. Over the coming chapters, you might run into words like *Sons of God, Zion, The Elect, The First Fruits, Overcomers,* and *The Bride.* All these are alternative names of *The Kingdom.*

The intent of the book is making "Milk" available to the spiritually immature and "Meat" for the more spiritually mature. For this reason, it might seem, at first, to be all over the place. However, as it develops, it all synchronizes harmoniously. With that said, two essential points are necessary for the reader to appreciate concerning the author's understanding of the purpose of life and existence, and why this book matters.

First, God created the Universe as a home for Man. It is man's permanent abode, not Heaven. Secondly, God created Man as a potential home for God. He is God's permanent abode, not Heaven. All that happened on earth in the past, and taking place now, is directly or indirectly actualizing that intention. This book should help the reader find the Kingdom of God within you. So, if someone was to ask, "where is the Kingdom?" We would respond by saying YOU are the Kingdom of God. (Lk. 17:20-21) (1Peter2:5).

The bible is full of allegories that indicate that man is the intended home of God. From Noah's Ark to Moses' Tabernacle and David's Tent to Solomon's Temple, all these edifices are symbolic of the real and permanent abode of God, Man himself. All these structures, except the Tent of David, had three dimensions or levels. David's Tent for God's Ark was the only one to which the worshipers could come directly and not need to pass through stages to have their petitions heard. The Ark of the Covenant was symbolic of God's presence. At the same time, the Tent of David and the structures mentioned previously were symbolic of the body of the Son of David, the Son of God, The Man Jesus Christ.

In that day will I raise up the tabernacle of David that is fallen, and close up the breaches thereof; and I will raise up his ruins, and I will build it as in the days of old (Am. 9:11) and (Acts. 15:16).

We begin by looking at the human condition and evolution of world history, from a theological as well as a teleological perspective. We will analyze some issues that relate to ethnicity, but not to demean or prejudice the reader in any way. Ethnicity and religion have been used for over a millennium to justify wars and exploitation. That said, no scholarly attempt to enlighten the minds of men can avoid these subjects if it seeks to be completely truthful and honest in approach.

THE HUMAN CONDITION

IF I HAD TO USE ONE WORD TO DESCRIBE THE HUMAN CONDITION, IT would be *Fragile*. We are so weak and fragile, yet we carry ourselves with the assurance and confidence that we know where we will be in the next five minutes. Our natural composition is so easily susceptible to sickness and disease, the same for our emotional state. Yet, we walk with the mask of certainty. Let us try to understand who we are.

Each person is a Soul; she has a spirit and inhabits a body. The Soul has four variants: the *Mind*, *Desire*, the *Will*, and the *Emotions*.

We are fragile beings here on earth in terms of our constitution. In character, we often hate one another or hurt and are hurt by one another. Paradoxically, we most often do not intend to harm or be harmed. Still, the vagaries of life throw up situations and circumstances beyond our control, thereby revealing our fragility to ourselves. The good things we intend to do, we find ourselves unable to do. The bad things we do not want to do, we find ourselves doing.

These actions and conditions can be debilitating and traumatic if we do not have an inner core that gives us the strength to overcome these challenges. Some of these hurts come from emotions and are not always physical. How devastating it is to have emotional or physical pain that you cannot explain or describe to another; but must suffer alone. The pain might be tolerable for a few years, but certainly not forever. Knowing that there could be a real person who can not only empathize, but also do something to change the situation is comforting and reassuring. It is about such a person I have chosen to write.

Let us begin by understanding what the bible teaches about the Soul. The Soul consists of four aspects; Mind, Desire, Will, and Emotion. Your *mind* is the aspect by which you seek to make sense of the phenomena you observe or experience in an abstract or apparent form. Scripture uses an *Eagle* to symbolize the *mind*. Whether we are looking, thinking, or perceiving, we use it to discern and interpret the world around us. Sometimes physical or psychological trauma knocks our minds off the usual orbits expected, and this will often lead to a poor mental state. Those on the outside might not notice the changes we experience in our minds. Still, in such a condition, we are a possible danger to ourselves and others. For this reason, scripture is given to us that expresses the will of God concerning our minds. *"For God hath not given us the spirit of fear; but of power, and of love, and of a sound mind"* (2 Tim. 1:7).

Your *Desire* is the aspect that can inspire you to want things. If not controlled, it pursues after vanities and lusts.

> *The leech has two daughters: Give and Give. There are three things that are never satisfied, four that never say, "Enough!": Sheol, the barren womb, land that is never satisfied with water, and fire that never says, "Enough"* (Prov. 30:15-16).

When used appropriately, it motivates us to achieve great things. Scripture uses *Man* to symbolize *Desire*. Man's desires are insatiable. Unlike the desires of brute beasts, man's can never be satisfied. Man's insatiable longing is by design. It can only find satisfaction when his creator inhabits the man. Desire is a necessary variant. Without it, you would not want to go out and do the things pleasing to God. You would not wish to start a business and contribute to the financial wellbeing of your family. You would not want much out of life.

Your *will* is the aspect that carries out the work of self-control. Old Testament scriptures use an Ox, and the New Testament uses a *Calf* to symbolize the Will. Without your will, you could not decide for Christ. You could not resist temptation. You would not CHOOSE to do the things you desire. *"For the good that I would I do not: but the evil which I would not, that I do. Now if I do that I would not, it is no more I that do it, but sin that dwelleth in me.* "(Rom. 7:19). Sin sometimes overpowers our will. In this situation, we can obtain deliverance by merely calling upon the name of Jesus for help.

Your *Emotion* is the final aspect of you. The *Lion* is symbolic of your *Emotions* in scripture. The image of the Lion represents passion and fervency. When not effectively managed, it can cause us to make rash decisions or do things we later come to regret. The emotions are that aspect of your nature that works you up when your favorite team is winning by a slight margin or losing by a considerable margin.

> *Be sober, be vigilant; because your adversary the devil, as a roaring lion, walketh about, seeking whom he may devour: Whom resist steadfast in the faith, knowing that the same afflictions are accomplished in your brethren that are in the world.* (1 Pet. 5:8-9)

WHO IS CHRIST?

MUCH WRITING EXISTS ABOUT JESUS CHRIST, AND MOST children could tell you he was a good man who lived many centuries ago. Those of Faith would say to you he was a holy man, or he died for their sins on a Cross 2000 years ago, or that he is coming soon to judge the earth. Some others would say he is a mythical figure who never really existed. But is a creation of the ecclesiastical hierarchy, to control the behavior of society, by holding his character out as an exemplar.

However, our question is not about who Jesus Christ was, but who is Christ. Every person that comes, or ever came into this world, has the essence of Christ in them. Christ is the essence of creation. He is the reason and the basis for the existence of everything. In some mysterious way, a person not rooted in Christ can symbolically be said not to exist.

> *For in Him all things were created, things in Heaven and on earth, visible and invisible, whether thrones or dominions or rulers or authorities. All things were created through Him and for Him. He is before all things, and in Him all things hold together (Col. 1:16-17).*

Every person reading this book has Christ in them. He is the Light that Lights up EVERY MAN that comes into the world. *"That was the true Light, which lighteth every man that cometh into the world"* (John 1:4-9). However, this light is something we avoid because our conscience does not vibrate at the same frequency that his light does. Through religion and social work, we perform all manner of good deeds to try to compensate for the wrong we see our life causing. Still, we can never seem to do enough to diminish the probing intensity of his light.

Only with a life that vibrates at the same intensity of frequency as his light, can we receive that certainty of peace and security. This peace and security are possible even with a conscience that vibrates at a different frequency if the Soul has received the lifeblood of Jesus Christ. It is possible to vibrate at the required frequency without much effort. It is my observation and conviction that this intensity can be obtained by:

- *Believing* in his incarnation as Jesus Christ,
- *Understanding* the necessity of his suffering. and
- *Proclaiming* the victory won thru his resurrection.

"That if thou shalt confess with thy mouth the Lord Jesus, and shalt believe in thine heart that God hath raised him from the dead, thou shalt be saved" (Rom.10:9). The apparent simplicity of this demand is what makes it seem so unbelievable.

Christ is the power of God made apparent, to uplift us from every challenging condition where we find ourselves. *"For I am not ashamed of the gospel of Christ: for it is the power of God unto salvation to everyone that believeth; to the Jew first, and also to the Greek"* (Rom 1:16). The next question is, Why? What evidence could we give to prove our assertion? As we go along in studying this book, you will discover things that will change, not only your perspective but your life and character also. It is this transformation of your life that will be my Observable evidence of the power of God.

This Faith in Christ of which I speak is not something attested to by just the New Testament Gospels. Before the existence of biblical Israel, Christ was revealed by the Spirit of God to other nations and peoples, though not as succinctly as he presents himself to us. The story about the Magi in the gospels is an indication of this. Also, the statements by Balaam, who was Edomite, when he prophesied about Christ, is more evidence of non-Israelite knowledge of Christ. *"I shall see him, but not now: I shall behold him, but not nigh: there shall come a Star out of Jacob, and a Sceptre shall rise out of Israel, and shall smite the corners of Moab, and destroy all the children of Sheth"* (Num 24:17). Even the story of Job is about a man who lived before Abraham. The observation of Nebuchadnezzar when he saw the "fourth man" in the fire is also evidence of the knowledge of Christ among the Babylonians (Dan. 3:24-25).

Most importantly, we must know that Faith in Christ is not optional, even for God (Heb. 11:1-3). Without him, God does not do any of the things he does, nor did because Christ is the Word of God. On the surface, this statement might seem blasphemous to those who see Christ as no more than a man. Yes, Jesus Christ is a man, but Christ is the aspect of God that creation can comprehend and see. No one can ever see God in his absolute totality as God, our Father. Every time we see him or the prophets of old saw him; Christ is the person seen. No one can see God in his totality; therefore, he appears to us in a stepped down power as the Son of God. The Son of God I.S. God. He is not a different person.

Philip saith unto him, Lord, shew us the Father, and it sufficeth us. Jesus saith unto him, Have I been so long time with you, and yet hast thou not known me, Philip? he that hath seen me hath seen the Father; and how sayest thou then, Shew us the Father? *John 14:8-9)

When Christ said he would send the Holy Spirit, he reiterated that it was HE himself returning in the person of the Holy Spirit.

And I will pray the Father, and he shall give you another Comforter, that he may abide with you for ever; Even the Spirit of truth; whom the world cannot receive, because it seeth him not, neither knoweth him: but ye know him; for he dwelleth with you, and shall be in you. I will not leave you comfortless: I will come to you. (John 14:16-18)

"All things were made by him; and without him was not anything made that was made" (Jn.1:3). *"In whom also we have obtained an inheritance, being predestinated according to the purpose of him who worketh all things after the counsel of his own will: That we should be to the praise of his glory, who first trusted in Christ"* (Eph.1:11-12). *"Now faith is the substance of things hoped for, the evidence of things not seen. For by it the elders obtained a good report"* (Heb.11:1).

"Through faith we understand that the worlds were framed by the Word of God, so that things which are seen were not made of things which do appear" (Heb. 11:1-3).

The same capability of Faith that God has is that which every human being has.

For I say, through the grace given unto me, to every man that is among you, not to think of himself more highly than he ought to think; but to think soberly, according as God hath dealt to every man the measure of Faith (Rom. 12:3).

The question is, in what do we put our faith? Do we put in the assurance that tomorrow will be worse than today? Or do we put it in the knowledge of what God has spoken? The only thing you have the power of changing is your destiny. Everything else, God will handle. This Faith in Christ is the substance that God used to create the Universe. Imagine what you can create with it.

When we say that Christ is "The Word" of God, we mean that he is the "Logos" or *"raison d 'être"* for everything that God does. God doesn't do anything without reason. We can rest assured that whatever it is that is happening in our lives is totally under the control of Christ.

SCIENCE AND FAITH

T HIS CHAPTER IS THE MOST DIFFICULT FOR ME TO WRITE, AS THE relevance of science and the understanding of it, as it relates to the person of Christ, is not a straightforward correlation to communicate. However, in times of old, Prophets and Kings used the expressions of nature around them to describe the glory of God. In these times of more knowledge and understanding of the phenomena of nature and its Science, we, too, should be able to see the glory of Christ in the most sublime realities of nature. We should also acknowledge its limitation to express the profound greatness of God in Christ adequately. The *Scientific Method* has been the tool by which scholastic theologians have learned and trained their inductees in the understanding of things spiritual and divine.

While this method of learning is not wrong in and of itself, the fact is that faith operates and motivates from a dimension that is beyond scientific observation. Since much of what we can understand about religion is written vastly in many holy books, I will concentrate more on describing the philosophical perspectives on Science. And how Christianity and other religions use it to understand spiritual phenomena. I will begin with spiritual and scientific viewpoints on how humans came to be on earth.

There are two Primary perspectives about how humans came to exist on earth. The first is the Evolutionary hypothesis, as popularized by Charles Darwin. The second is the hypothesis (as offered by most religious people throughout history). That some Prime Mover, God, created all things, with man as his extraordinary creature above all others. Generally, people have a perspective that combines both in some manner. I hold on to the position that God did create the earth and ***man*** in six days. And just as he formed Adam as an adult man, not a baby, he also created the Universe as a mature entity millions of years old within those six days. The question is how we measure a Creation Day. There were no Sun, Moon, or Stars for the first three biblical days.

The proponents of evolution can offer only circumstantial evidence for the validity of their theory. The very nature of man and his higher morals stand as evidence of a being more complicated than an animal. I intend to demonstrate that man is more than a natural being, and that there exists a fundamental difference between Man and Beast. Namely, that man is spiritual and at once natural. He is regulated by Conscience and Reason, with a consciousness that never dies. For example, mankind universally abhors any sexual relationships between immediate family members. Animals do not. When mankind engages in such behavior, we observe an increase in diseases among the offspring of such relationships. These diseases are a consequence of inbreeding. There are no similar problems among animals, which is evidence that man is something much more than a higher primate. We should begin with the explanation of modern science as to the origin of the universe and man. Most of what modern "science" teaches about the beginning of the Universe is mere speculation at best. The most popular of these is the so-called big bang theory.

The evolutionary hypothesis is the dominant "scientific" perspective across the world today. Even though evolution is still a "Theory," its adherents teach it as scientific fact. Evolution was a theory alluded to at first by many Greek philosophers such as Aristotle and by others more recently, such as Carl Linnaeus and Erasmus Darwin, grandfather of the most famous disciple of this school of thought. Carl Linnaeus proposed the theory of evolution 100 years before Charles Darwin. However, there are some crucial differences between Charles Darwin's approach, and that of Linnaeus, the reconciliation of their positions is not the intended purpose of this book.

The evolutionary hypothesis teaches that due to genetic mutations, adaptation, and natural selection, we and other living creatures have evolved into what we are. This evolution occurred through a need for survival and the continuity of those aspects of our nature that are most beneficial to us (Darwin, C. 1859). The full title of Darwin's book is **"The origin of species, by means of natural selection, or the preservation of favoured races in the struggle for life."**

Darwin concentrated his ideas of "Race" mostly on plants and animals. However, in his second book, The descent of man, he says, "*The civilized (White) races of man will almost certainly exterminate and replace, the savage races throughout the world.*" Most proponents of the Darwinian theory do not often discuss the influence such scientific perspectives have had on social policies of Governments. Imperialism, Fascism, and Communism relied upon the ideas of Darwin as evidence of the need for their programs of starvation, ethnic cleansing, and the use of violence in governance.

The writings of Charles Darwin so enthralled Karl Marx that he resorted to the works often as corroboration of his socio/economic and political theories on Class structure and conflict. Even though the two men never met, Karl Marx sent a free copy of one of his books to Darwin. Fredrich Engels, the ideological sidekick of Marx, described the similarities between the works of Darwin and Marx during his funeral oration for the Late Karl Marx. Simply put, the philosophies of Imperialism, Marxism, and Darwinism, as it relates to human beings, are cut from the same cloth. They have justified the barbarism of ethnic cleansings and political killings all over the world by claiming the long term benefits of their actions will be evident in time. The current educational system and the economic system, referred to as Capitalism, are also based on this theory. Capitalism (a kind of Science) is not *Free Enterprise Economics*, just as modern schooling is not education.

The alternative view, which I subscribe to, is that God created every Genus of Plant and Animal, however over time, different species have come forth from these Plants and Animals. For example, a Horse, a Zebra, and a Donkey are of the same Genus, while the three are different species. Also, an African Elephant and an Asian Elephant are the same Genus, but not the same species. So, when it says in the bible that God told Noah to take two of all unclean creatures, and seven of all clean animals, it was referring to the Genus (Kind) and not to every beast. For example, the dogs we have today, like German Shepherds or Rottweilers are the same species. Still, the Dingo is considered a different species but the same Genus (Kind). In rare instances, animals of the same Genus but different species can interbreed. In the case of human beings, we are all the same species, we can adapt but cannot evolve, except spiritually. Our Souls do the evolving, and not our bodies. Even though our bodies might *adapt* to differentiation in the environment, we do not *evolve* physically into a different species on a genetic level.

The material universe (Universe means Single Word), which we inhabit, is itself mutable and not a tangible essence of itself. It receives its tangibility from the fact that it was spoken into existence by God in the person of Jesus Christ. What I mean is that by the Faith of God, the very Universe that we see has come into being. It is not eternal and only exists by the sheer Faith of God in his Word. It will pass away in due time. (2 Pet. 3:7). Just as God, we give form and substance to impressions that appear to us mentally, creating for ourselves the eternal reality we will have. A universe of harmony and everlasting life, or a cosmos of disharmony and everlasting torment. We all are in the process of creating our eternal abode. By faith, each person relates to the Universe she creates as a tangible object. Her mind communicates with the projection in this manner based on conditioning.

The Apostle Paul says to us in the Book of Hebrews:

> *Now faith is the substance of things hoped for, the evidence of things not seen. For by it the elders obtained a good report. Through faith we understand that the worlds were framed by the Word of God, so that things which are seen were not made of things which do appear* (Heb.11:1-3)

What we touch is not made from what we see. It is by faith that we have certainty that we can walk on the earth and not sink through or walk on water and sink through. When Jesus came, he sought to show us that these "laws" were in our minds, as exemplified in his teaching to Peter on how to walk on water. Every human being born into this life has as much Faith as God himself does. The question is, how do we use this faith?

> *For I say, through the grace given unto me, to every man that is among you, not to think of himself more highly than he ought to think; but to think soberly, according as God hath dealt to every man the measure of Faith* (Rom. 12:3).

Depending on your spiritual maturity, you might not use your faith to the degree your neighbor can. When Jesus and his disciples were in a little boat, a storm came, and the Apostles became scared for their lives. The elements seemed to be beyond their control. They noticed Jesus was asleep unworried by the tumult. In a panic, they cried to him to do something. He woke up and SPOKE to the sea, and it became calm. (Mark 4:35-41).

The bible quotes in the prior paragraph precede these statements by Nobel Prize-winning scientists Niels Bohr and Max Planck. According to Bohr,

"Everything we call real is made of things that cannot be regarded as real." Planck said **"I regard Consciousness as fundamental. I regard matter as derivative from Consciousness. We cannot get behind Consciousness."**

The modern understanding of the link between matter and Consciousness is profound since thousands of years before modern Science; the scriptures had stated that nature was subject to the human mind, and that *"the things we see are not made from things that do appear"* (Heb. 11:13).

Laws of Science that operate predictably at surface levels do not function with the same regularity at quantum levels. Which is a fact natural science researchers understood for the past one hundred years. For this reason, in modern physics, the Laws of Motion, Gravity, Electromagnetism, and Weak/Strong Force theory might not apply at quantum levels. Further, in Quantum physics, Science has demonstrated that Physical objects such as Neutrinos can be at multiple places AT THE SAME TIME. (This concept is the "Super Position State." According to Pais, H. (2014), "how a particle reacts to an influence can be predicted only in terms of probabilities. But this is not the end of the story: UNLESS THE EFFECT ON THE PARTICLE IS ACTUALLY OBSERVED, ALL POSSIBLE CONSEQUENCES SEEM TO BE REALIZED SIMULTANEOUSLY. PARTICLES CAN RESIDE IN TWO DIFFERENT LOCATIONS AT ONCE!"

The philosophic school of Democritus influences modern Science. Democritus was the philosopher who coined the idea that everything was composed of little things called Atoms. In between, them was nothing but a Void referred to as space. The Word Atom derives from the Greek Word Atoma, which means indivisible. Contrary to this school of thought was the Socratic school, which taught that reality was imperceptible to the ungifted mind. The things we see "appear" to be the things we do not see, but they are not the thing they purport to be. In the words of Plato, a student of Socrates, behind this realm of perception that we experience, lies the real world. The real world is a world of "Forms" In this world of Forms is the essence of everything we perceive in our minds but can never experience in our lives. Everything we see with our natural eyes is "Participating" in attempting to mimic the real thing that lies beyond the veil of human perception. So, for example, when you look at a chair, it is not a chair. It is wood participating in the Form of a Chair. For this reason, over time, the chair will experience decay and entropy, transforming into something else through human agency or decay.

This Socratic/Platonic method of thinking influenced the early Church fathers after the era of the Apostles. Many early church fathers believed so much in the ideas of Socrates and Plato that some people called them Neo-Platonists. The very philosophies of Plato and Socrates permeated modern Christianity and influenced Science up until the era of the 19th Century. In the 19th Century, the ideas of Democritus came back and became the dominant mode of understanding our world by scientists. The very concept of "Heaven" as a place that this earth resembles but in an imperfect way, is not an idea from the bible, but Socrates, as handed to us by his student, Plato.

Yes, the bible speaks about Heaven, but not with the idea that most Christians postulate about it. There are no physical "streets of Gold," for example. Even though the bible does speak about "A Street of Gold" (Rev. 21:21), it is not referring to a Street like you, and I see in any town today. Jesus himself is likened unto a street, *"I am the WAY, the truth and the life"* (John 14:6). So God uses symbolic icons in the bible to communicate a message to the initiates about his ideas and plans. The unlearned in the mysteries of God utilizes the Socratic/Platonist method to their self-deception, trying to decipher the Mysteries handed down to those initiated into the Order of Melchizedek (The Order God established).

The church uses the Socratic/Platonist method of analysis and hence conflicts not only with modern Science but the revelatory pattern of God. I am not saying that modern science is correct, or in consonance with God. As we have observed, the Socratic ideas are related to another current scientific method; Quantum Theory. The Socratic/Platonist Method and Quantum science generally agree that what we See, take on or "participate" in the *form* that exists in an infinite realm. We see with our natural eyes its shadow. The primary difference is that Quantum Science says that by observation, we can affect the state of the object. So those who control perception, control reality.

In contrast, the Socratic/Platonist method says we are unable to do so because a thing is in and of itself a Thing. The Socratic/Platonist method states we can only observe an object, but we cannot change its form. What we can change is our mind, and if it's transformed, then we will have the capability of understanding a thing as it is. To the Socratic/Platonist, we need depth perception in the mental state, not just the physical. One way to explain it is to use the example of two people walking towards each other while a third person observes. Suppose you have two people walking towards each other from opposite directions while you gaze at them from afar to the side. Without a perception of depth, you will be unable to anticipate that they would walk past each other because they are at different distances from you. Only when they are within the same distance from beneath you, you would expect their bumping into each other. Seeing things from the Spiritual/Metaphysical perspective allows you to have this depth perception.

Newtonian Science does not subscribe to the concept of "flux" that Quantum science does. Quantum science grants that an object can manifest in multiple spaces at the same time; Newtonian Science says that at best, the item is being observed at different times simultaneously. To the Newtonian scientist, it is incredulous that a physical object could inhabit multiple spaces at the same time. However, recent experiments indicate that they might be wrong: matter can occupy numerous spaces simultaneously! Phenomena are incomprehensible using Newtonian Science or Religion since Newtonian Science restricts observation of Force and Matter to the observable and, religion limits our understanding of spiritual realities by dogma.

So, the reader might ask what this has to do with the Word of God or Faith in Christ. The answer is simple. Jesus Christ IS a physical man who can be in multiple places at the same time. He is not dead. In the book of John, he said precisely that *"And no man has ascended into heaven except he who came from heaven; I myself who is in heaven"* (John 3:13). According to (1 John 3:2), we shall be like Jesus when we shall SEE him. The emphasis is on observation. The fact that we live in a material body is no limitation. So theoretically, according to quantum science, the claim that a physical being can be in multiple places at the same time is not improbable. Also, the scriptures teach us that a time is coming when we shall have our physical bodies transformed into a body like that which Jesus has now (Phil. 3:21).

The Apostle Paul himself was caught up into another realm, possibly in his physical body, as Elijah was.

> *I knew a man in Christ above fourteen years ago, (whether in the body, I cannot tell; or whether out of the body, I cannot tell: God knoweth;) such an one caught up to the third Heaven. And I knew such a man, (**whether in the body, or out of the body, I cannot tell: God knoweth;** How that he was caught up into paradise, and heard unspeakable words, which it is not lawful for a man to utter* (2 Corinthians 12:2-4).
> This is an example of Quantum Teleportation.

Quantum physics indicates that this is quite possible for a physical object. Why then would we find it impossible to believe the same could be true of the man Jesus Christ? *"And no man hath ascended up to Heaven, but he that came down from Heaven, even the Son of man **which is in heaven** "*(Jn. 3:13). According to this scripture, Jesus was in Heaven at the same time while he was on earth. Being in two places simultaneously is what is meant by "Let us make man in our own image <u>and</u> likeness." It is a process that began in the first chapter of Genesis and continues today. We are working alongside Him to finish the job on ourselves. According to Paul: *"Who shall change our vile body, that it may be fashioned like unto his glorious body, according to the working whereby he is able even to subdue all things unto himself"* (Phil. 3:21).

This transformation of our bodies to become like Christ's body is similar to the scientific concept of Quantum Entanglement. Though Jesus is in heaven, my very essence and his have become entangled that wherever he is, I am, and wherever I am he is. Whatever he does, I do. *"Then answered Jesus and said unto them, Verily, verily, I say unto you, The Son can do nothing of himself, but what he seeth the Father do: for what things soever he doeth, these also doeth the Son likewise"* (John 5:19).

In conclusion, let us talk about the COVID-19 Virus of 2020 because it is a phenomenon that will be with us for a long time. A virus is different from a Bacteria in that Viruses are not living organisms even though they have a genetic code. According to the World Health Organization (WHO), "the Virus that causes COVID-19 is in a family of Viruses called Coronaviridae". We do not use Antibiotics to cure Viruses, except in the instance in which a patient contracts a bacterial infection while receiving treatment for a virus. Antibiotics treat the bacteria, not the illness.

Viruses are an efficient means of conducting biological warfare, both overtly and covertly. Many countries have laboratories that specialize in weaponizing known viruses. The laboratory in China where the COVID-19 is assumed to have originated from was involved in such research. There is every possibility that its release was intentional, to serve as a conduit to bring about socio-economic and political change in the world. The suspicion does not necessarily mean that the Chinese Government or any other Government, for that matter, was directly involved in its release. There are many non-state actors now that control and shape policy and opinion worldwide. Such persons have the power to do things that previously seemed impossible.

The reaction and hysteria in response to the virus seem to have served a purpose that is still unfolding. The believers in God should be prayerful because it seems we are living in the time that Jesus referred to as: *"Men's hearts failing them for fear of the things coming upon the earth"* (Lk. 21:26). The virus has served as a useful tool to change social behavior and patterns, to usher in laws that contradict the Word of God. Most startling of all is the power granted to governments by a frightened public to ban group gatherings from worshiping the creator of the Universe. The primary purpose for which he created us I.S. to worship him. Any attempt by believers to hold a view contrary to the orthodox panacea is immediately delegitimized, as "Conspiracy Theory."

Just as Darwinism is upheld, as THE scientific fact of creation, so the orthodox response to the COVID-19 pandemic was placed high and dangerous enough to give governments worldwide dictatorial powers. The intent seems to be to insist that no person can travel without showing evidence of having received a vaccine for the virus. I believe that anyone that feels she wants a vaccine should get it. People who do not take the vaccine are only dangerous to themselves. No one explained why we punish those who refuse the vaccine when they are of no threat to those who willingly take the vaccine. We know that the bible says: *"He causes all, both small and great, rich and poor, free and slave, to receive a Mark on their right hand or their foreheads, and that no one may buy or sell except one who has the Mark or the name of the beast, or the number of his name"* (Rev. 13:16-17).

Of course, the scriptures are referring primarily to spiritual *Marks* and *Numbers* and not just physical. However, we ought not to discard the possibility of a dual service of the scriptures, considering the "manifold wisdom of God." The believers worldwide should be wise and choose for themselves if God has spoken to them as individuals to stay away from a group meeting or not. They should, under no circumstance, obey any government edict or law that runs contrary to the moral laws of God. I am not referring to the ceremonial laws of scriptures. If it becomes necessary for the believers to go underground to worship, then so be it. Never under any circumstance should violence be used except in the instance of immediate danger of loss of life from extrajudicial killing.

We discussed the two prominent schools of Science and the Socratic/Platonist perspective of modern religion. Christ can neither be understood by the scientific method nor by the philosophic process of popular religion. We insist that he is who the scriptures say he is, and demonstrate the value that faith in him has to society. Quantum Science indicates that matter can occupy multiple spaces at the same time. It appears that objects can also co-occur in various times (as espoused by Albert Einstein's space-time relativity principles). We looked at these subjects to see the scientific probability that some of the natural transformations we expect to come upon creation in the future are scientifically possible.

A BRIEF HISTORY OF RELIGION

MOST OF US DO NOT UNDERSTAND THE MEANING OF THE WORD *religion*. Religion simply means "the process of tying or binding again that which is loosed." So, religion is a form of bondage. The prefix 'Re' means to do again. The latter part of the word "ligion" comes from the Latin word "Legare," which means to bind. So, to "Re-Legare" means to bind again. Once a person obtains the liberating knowledge of Christ, the anti-Christ system (*Religion*) looks for a way to get her "bound" in one form of "Christian" Religion or another. Before we look more into the details concerning this, lets first look at the development of man, and consequently the evolution of religion.

Figure 8 – Nsude Pyramids near Enugu Nigeria, which were destroyed by the British Colonialists

Initially, all human beings were African. The most ancient rituals conducted in all major religions in the world find their origins in Africa. Before people inhabited the rest of the world, Africans practiced sacrificial rites and other rituals (including the absolution of sins). There is reason to believe that the only humans on earth at the beginning resembled the modern African. It is reasonable that the first men in the bible were Negroid, when we consider that only within this race of humanity, are all the genetic markers in other ethnicities found. Genetics is profound because it shows that in the average African is the genetic makeup of all races on earth. However, no other ethnicity has all the genetic markers that the Africans have. One phenotypical example of this is the diversity found in Central Africa. There you find the tallest people in the world (Sudanic) and the shortest (Twa) mistakenly referred to as pygmies. Over time the Africans migrated out of Africa and *adapted* to the different regions of the world they traveled. It is from these people we inherit the first inclinations of religion and superstition. Their rock paintings and art preserved in the caves of the Sahara reveal this to us. The step Pyramids of Egypt are the oldest in the world and preceded the great pyramid at Giza. Scientists found replicas of these step pyramids in Nigeria, but by the 19th Century, European colonialists, seeking treasure, destroyed them. Fortunately, we have pictures of these ancient pyramids in Nigeria before they were destroyed (see Figure 8).

The zenith of this religion occurred on the Nile, where the ancient Kingdom of Egypt flourished. From there, it spread to the rest of the world. First to Babylon/Sumer, and then to Persia/Indus Valley. Almost all modern religions are a variation of some Egyptian myth. Even the Muslim, Judaics, Buddhists, Hindu, and Catholics of today borrowed their prayer patterns from the Ancient Egyptians and Babylonians.

Ideally, the subject of the racial identity of the first humans would be unnecessary when discussing spirituality. But because of the influence race has had on the Religion and Faith of people, we must refute, with understanding, some of the racial myths imposed on adherents using twisted scriptures. The most popular of these myths is the so-called *curse of Ham* (though the scriptures never cursed Ham). This myth was first propagated by Middle Eastern Judaic and Muslim scholars, as well as Christian Europeans to justify the slave trade. The Trans-Saharan slave trade, which predated the Transatlantic slave trade and continued well beyond the 19th Century, was the most gruesome of all.

The earliest bible and theological schools in Europe and America also taught: God cursed black people, and enslaving and forcefully converting blacks to Christianity was their obligation. The same principle was the foundation of the Mohammedan slave trade. The Judaic merchants who owned more than fifty percent of the slave ships in the trans-Atlantic slave trade also had these teachings from their holy book The Talmud. The fact is that these were doctrines espoused to achieve two things. First, it justified a morally unsound business practice before the eyes of the common folk. Secondly, it gave *cognitive dissonance* to help assuage the conscience of those who participated in the barbaric Trans-Saharan and Trans-Atlantic Slave trade.

The Mormons also taught their adherents that blacks could not be sure of salvation nor serve as Priests because they had sinned in a previous life. The bias against blacks was the official belief system of the so-called *"Church of Jesus Christ of the Latter-Day Saints."* However, in the mid-seventies, the American government threatened to pull the "church's" non-profit status. Suddenly, their "Prophet" got a "revelation" that blacks could now be Priests and enter Heaven when they died. Throughout this period of discrimination, some blacks continued to be dedicated members of this organization. Go figure!

The Catholic Pope Nicholas V was the first Pope to authorize the perpetual enslavement of Non-Christian peoples by the European powers. He ordered this through the Papal Bull *Romanus Pontifex* on January 5th, 1455. In 1493 Pope Alexander VI expanded the rights of slavery granted to European monarchs as a need for labor in the New World increased. These are historical and documented facts that were an attempt to dehumanize people using the garb of religion.

By the end of the 16th Century, England was under the rule of Queen Elizabeth 1st (the sister of the so-called "Bloody Mary"). She had entered a close political relationship with the King of Morocco, Mohammed Al-Mansur. Most historians describe the political and military alliance between them as one of convenience against Spain. However, this is somewhat disingenuous. We know that Queen Elisabeth explicitly stated that the weapons, she supplied Morocco were only for use against Christian nations that were at war with England. So, then the question would be, who did Morocco need to fight with all those weapons obtained from England. The answer is Songhai. Songhai was the last West African Kingdom that stretched from Senegal to Nigeria. A succession of Muslim and Pagan Kings led Songhai with harmonious respect for each individual's religious freedom. It also had the great universities of Sankore, Timbuktu, and Gao. It also controlled the Salt Mines in the Sahel, which had an abundance of Saltpeter (Nitrate), a necessary ingredient for Gunpowder. It is by the supply of the Canons from England that Morocco was able to destroy Songhai and carve out economic interests in West Africa for itself and England.

The significance of this, when studied in detail, will reveal that while the West Africans considered the Moroccans to be brothers in religion, the Moroccans did not understand the relationship to be so. The phrase "travel as far as Timbuktu" comes from the reality that since Songhai had the best scholars and scholarly works in the world at the time, Moroccans and others traveled there for education. The influence of Songhai extended down to the areas referred to today as the Niger Delta area of Nigeria. Nigeria almost changed its name to Songhai at the beginning of its Independence from Great Britain. With the destruction of Songhai, Morocco and other Arab states began the plunder of West Africa for Slaves as they had done in East and North Africa. They became the arrowhead into the hinterland of West Africa for the capture of slaves bound for the Trans-Atlantic slave trade. Unfortunately, history today teaches that most of the slaves were exported from West Africa by fellow Africans, which is historically false.

Indeed, there were African slave raiders in the coast. Still, their numbers were nothing compared to the number of invading Arab and Pule horseback riders (the Pule/ Fulatta were a mixed race of Arab and African). This military cavalry served as the spearhead for the Arab conquest of Africa and historically saw themselves as distinct from West Africans. The intermarriage between them and the pure West Africans has reduced this distinction over time). They ravished villages and towns in the Sahel for hundreds of years after the fall of Timbuktu for onward deportation to the coast and final sale to the waiting European ships. This disregard for commonality in religion between the Arabs and their fellows of black ancestry is a condition that most black Muslim scholars overlook for reasons unknown to this writer.

The adherents of the Abrahamic religions conspired to disregard the tenets of their faith when it comes to making a profit at the expense of their black Christian, Judaic, or Islamic brothers of faith. Religion has often been a powerful tool for good but has done little to assuage the greed of its adherents.

The European, Islamic, and Judaic scholars turned the biblical story (where Moses' sister and brother being angry that Moses had married an "Ethiopian" woman) into a racial tool. It did not matter that Moses was an Egyptian in looks and that the bible tells us that Egyptians and Ethiopians were the same.

> *Princes shall come out of Egypt; Ethiopia shall soon stretch out her hands unto God" (Ps. 68:31)." Are ye not as children of the Ethiopians unto me, O children of Israel? saith the LORD. Have not I brought up Israel out of the land of Egypt? and the Philistines from Caphtor, and the Syrians from Kir? (Am. 9:7-2).*

Also (2 Kings 19:1-37) tells us of how God used the Ethiopians to save Israel from Assyria. The adherents of the three Abrahamic religions insisted on interpreting this story as one of racial disdain by Moses' family, rather than what it was: an ethnic bias against an Ethiopian woman. As the scripture mentioned above show, the Israelites considered the Ethiopians to be their brothers. The next few paragraphs will give a more concise version of the event so we can lay the myth to rest.

The Israelites had been in Egypt during some period of the Dynastic era. According

to the Egyptians themselves, the Egyptians originated from Uganda. According to the Egyptians: *"We came from the beginning of the Nile, where the god Hapi dwells at the foothills of the mountains of the moon"* (Papyrus of Hunefer, London Museum). If Moses had looked any different from the Egyptians of that period, how could Pharaoh's daughter have claimed him as hers? The simple fact of the matter was that Moses' sister and brother had no such racial consciousness. They were merely concerned that Moses had married a "foreign" woman contrary to the Laws that he had set. However, religious leaders used this spin to make people believe that it had something to do with skin color. They conveniently skipped the part where it said God punished Moses' sister for speaking against Moses by turning her skin white.

And Miriam and Aaron spake against Moses because of the Ethiopian woman whom he had married: for he had married an Ethiopian woman. And they said, Hath the LORD indeed spoken only by Moses? hath he not spoken also by us? And the LORD heard it. (Now the man Moses was very meek, above all the men which were upon the face of the earth.) And the LORD spake suddenly unto Moses, and unto Aaron, and unto Miriam, Come out ye three unto the tabernacle of the congregation. And they three came out. And the LORD came down in the pillar of the cloud, and stood in the door of the tabernacle, and called Aaron and Miriam: and they both came forth. And he said, Hear now my words: If there be a prophet among you, I the LORD will make myself known unto him in a vision, and will speak unto him in a dream. My servant Moses is not so, who is faithful in all mine house. With him will I speak mouth to mouth, even apparently, and not in dark speeches; and the similitude of the LORD shall he behold: wherefore then were ye not afraid to speak against my servant Moses? And the anger of the LORD was kindled against them; and he departed. And the cloud departed from off the tabernacle; and, behold, Miriam became leprous, white as snow: and Aaron looked upon Miriam, and, behold, she was leprous. And Aaron said unto Moses, Alas, my lord, I beseech thee, lay not the sin upon us, wherein we have done foolishly, and wherein we have sinned. Let her not be as one dead, of whom the flesh is half consumed when he cometh out of his mother's womb. And Moses cried unto the LORD, saying, Heal her now, O God, I beseech thee. And the LORD said unto Moses, If her father had but spit in her face, should she not be ashamed seven days? let her be shut out from the camp seven days, and after that let her be received in again. And Miriam was shut out from the camp seven days: and the people journeyed not till Miriam was brought in again (Num. 12:10).

This account was about the wife of Moses being from a foreign tribe. It had nothing to do with race as the Israelites were indeed not phenotypically different from the Ethiopians.

Let us dismantle another myth perpetuated by adherents of the Abrahamic religions: the mythical "curse of Ham." Noah and his three sons, Shem, Japheth, and Ham. They were all similar in hue since they had the same mother. Based on what we know from anthropological evidence, they would have resembled Africans. This assertion is corroborated by Science, which places the origin of man to be Africa. It is also an acknowledged scientific and anthropological fact that today, Africans have 100% Human gene type. At the same time, other "races" carry just some of all the genes carried by Africans, which is evidence of paternity. Therefore, if indeed we did descend from the three sons of Noah, it would have to be that the Africans are most representative of their phenotype.

I encourage the reader to do a personal academic search on the topic of human genetic ancestry because the roots of racism and justified eugenics is traceable to this myth of the *Hamitic curse*. Not only so, but the very idea of a "God Chosen Nation" in modern times owes more of its origin to this phenomenon rather than any appeal to the biblical anthology.

According to biblical history, as multiplied on the face of the earth, they wanted to create a centralized authority that would keep them in proximity to each other (e.g., the tower of Babel). They intended to build "a City" AND "a Tower" to prevent scattering upon the face of the earth, which violated God's intent. So, even before they could begin building the tower, God limited their communication capabilities. Hence they could no longer understand each other and cooperate in the contrarian venture. This confusion forced them to separate from each other and populate the entire earth with its different climatic conditions. These variations in climate *contributed* to the difference in the tone of different races on the planet today. All this occurred before the forming of continents, as mentioned in the bible (Gen. 10:25).

Now, even though God had wiped out all humankind except Noah and his seven family members, Sin continued to plague humanity. An alternative means of delivering man from the bondage of Sin, with its attendant fear of death needed introduction. So, after some time, Abraham, a man from the Chaldean region of Ur, had his compliance with God's will tested by God. His obedience opened a spiritual portal legitimizing the coming of Jesus to save humankind.

Abraham opened the portal with his simple act of faith. He BELIEVED that God could kill his Son and raise him again from the dead. When tried, he obeyed the voice of God by offering this Son on an altar. The timely intervention of God's angel saved the life of Isaac, and this act gave Abraham the title "Friend of God." It was by this same attitude of Faith that God would justify and save humankind from eternal death. However, it would still take a few more centuries before humanity would be ready for the message of "Salvation through faith":

The descendants of Abraham were Ishmael, Isaac, and their brothers and sisters. *"Then again Abraham took a wife, and her name was Keturah. And she bare him Zimran, and Jokshan, and Medan, and Midian, and Ishbak, and Shuah"* (Gen. 25:1-2). Based on the African tradition that gives priority to the first Son of the MARRIED wife, Isaac was the primary heir over his elder brother, Ishmael. Unfortunately, today much myth has arisen among theologians and scholars as to the peoples who are the direct descendants of these two. Sadly, all claims to blood descent are completely inauthentic myths.

Isaac had two sons, Esau and Jacob. These two brothers had the same mother, but we would see the same exchange of birthright that occurred under Abraham, occur under Isaac. The question to hold in mind is, could there be a more symbolic meaning to this substitution of the first for the second two times? More on this later.

Jacob used guile and conspiracy to obtain the birthright of the firstborn from his brother. Esau, his brother, did not fully appreciate the value of the inheritance and flippantly awarded it to his younger brother in a moment of hunger. He accepted his brother's condition that he relinquish his birthright for some of Jacob's food.

When eventually Isaac died, Jacob inherited the birthright of the first Son. Esau was angry when he understood the consequence of what he had done, but it was too late. What was the inheritance? The privilege to have the Messiah manifest in the world through him. That is the same birthright some of us seek today but in a different manner.

It is important to note that during the period after Noah, we have the first documented civilization called the Maa Confederacy (Winters, C. 2013). It would be followed by another of Ham's descendants, Mizrahim (Egypt), even though it continued to exist concurrently with Egypt. This information is necessary because we need to follow the trajectory of civilization as it co-occurs with the Patriarchs. It allows us to contextualize their decisions and the challenges they would face. For example, we know that Ab-Ra-Ham came into Egypt (Sometimes referred to as the land of Ham) with his wife Sarah and that it was already a flourishing civilization. He had not yet learned about circumcision, even though we know that the Egyptians and Cushites were already practicing circumcision. What influences might his stay in Egypt have had on him? Their chief Deity was Ptah, from whom we derive the English Word Father.

Jacob had twelve sons from his two wives and two concubines. His son Joseph was sold into slavery by his jealous brothers. Still, this wicked act of theirs turned out to be the crowning opportunity for Joseph because he grew to become Prime Minister of the most powerful Empire in the world; Egypt.

According to the bible, Jacob migrated into Egypt with his sons AND HIS SONS' SONS:

> And Jacob rose up from Beersheba: and the sons of Israel carried Jacob their father, and their little ones, and their wives, in the wagons which Pharaoh had sent to carry him. And they took their cattle, and their goods, which they had gotten in the land of Canaan, and came into Egypt, Jacob, and all his seed with him: His sons, and his sons' sons with him, his daughters, and his sons' daughters, and all his seed brought he with him into Egypt (Gen.46:5-7).

The migration account is essential because it gives us an indication of exactly how long the children of Israel were in Egypt. It certainly was not up to 400 years. The main reason being that Jacob was 130 years old when he migrated to Egypt, and he journeyed with Levi and Levi's Son, Kohath. Kohath was the father of Amram, and grandfather of Aaron and Moses, "the sons of Amram and Jochebed," which demonstrates that Moses was only two generations removed from Levi, the Son of Jacob. The Israelites were not in Egypt for 400 years. Even the Holy Ghost tells us so in Galatians:

> Now to Abraham and his seed were the promises made. He saith not, And to seeds, as of many; but as of one, And to thy seed, which is Christ. And this I say, that the covenant, that was confirmed before of God in Christ, the law, which was four hundred and thirty years after, cannot disannul, that it should make the promise of none effect (Gal. 3:16-17)

and·

> Now the sojourning of the children of Israel, who dwelt in Egypt, was four hundred and thirty years. And it came to pass at the end of the four hundred and thirty years, even the

selfsame day it came to pass, that all the hosts of the LORD went out from the land of Egypt (Ex. 12:40-41)

Galatians and Exodus accounts of the children of Israel are not in conflict. The scriptures count the sojourn of Israel from the time of Abraham, not from the entry of Jacob into Egypt, which is the esoteric meaning of "400 years." The period from the birth of Isaac to God giving the law to Moses was considerably less than 400 years. The statement in Galatians is significant to understanding exactly who the nation was, which God said would spend "400" years in Captivity. It was not the natural people of Israel in the bible who went into Egypt with Jacob. They were just symbolic of True Israel. The true Israel will be the nation that enters the *Kingdom of God*:

> *Not as though the Word of God hath taken none effect. <u>For they are not all Israel, which are of Israel</u>: Neither, because they are the seed of Abraham, are they all children: but, In Isaac shall thy seed be called. That is, they which are the children of the flesh, these are not the children of God: but the children of the promise are counted for the seed (Rom. 9:6-8).*

Earlier, we mentioned the first anthropologically dated civilization to have been the Maa civilization of Central Africa. After Maa came the Pre-Dynastic Egyptian culture, and then dynastic Egypt, following Egypt was Babylon, of which we will devote a little more information. After Babylon came the great powers of Persia, followed by Greece, and finally Rome. Of course, there have been many great Empires after Rome, but we are primarily concerned with BCE Empires at this stage. There were other great powers in the world during the height of these civilizations (i.e., the Assyrians, the Hittites, and the Cushites, among others). However, apart from the Cushites, none of these other powers left us any strong legacy as a Civilization.

It is essential to know that pre-dynastic Egypt existed for thousands of years before Dynastic Egypt and recorded names and deeds of its Kings and heroes. The main reason why scholars never include it as a civilization is that they do not consider some of what they said about their earlier lifespans logical. For example, they claimed their kings lived some extraordinarily long lives. They were living to ages like 500 or 600 years old, which seems unrealistic for scholars. However, bible scholars can affirm that the holy books claim pre-flood heroes like Methuselah and Noah also lived extraordinarily long lives.

The first account of the works of the Islamic Prophet Muhammad was not documented until about 800 C.E. Considering that he is supposed to have died in about 630 C.E., for almost 200 years, the only information about him and his revelation was information handed down by oral tradition. The Arab Saracens conquered parts of the Persian and Byzantine Empires to establish Arab domination of North Africa, Spain, and Persia. The Saracens do not mention Muhammad until about 800 C.E. Many people believe that the Arab conquests were synonymous with Islamic conquest. However, all the evidence seems to point to a non-Islamic Arab conquest of the regions mentioned above. The Arabs appear to have adopted Islam as a State religion much later. At least 150 years after the death of Muhammad. Even the conquest of Jerusalem by the Arabs has no evidence of the army being religious. The coins and literature of that period show no acknowledgment of the Religion of Islam.

Interestingly, the very earliest Mosques (after the Arabs had adopted Islam as the state religion) faced Petra in Jordan. That ancient city fits the description ascribed to "Mecca" in the Koran. (*Gibson, D. 2017*). Petra exists to this day as a popular tourist destination. The account given of Mecca in the Quran has a resemblance more of Petra than of modern Mecca. The Abbasids Dynasty of Islam was the first to move the holy shrine of Islam to what is today called Mecca. They were fleeing from the Umayyad when they set up base in Arabia.

Concerning Christ, the Quran acknowledges him as the Great Prophet/Messiah, who is to rule the world at the end of time. The Quran refers to him as "Isa Almasihu." Some crucial differences between what the bible and the Quran teach about Christ are significant enough for us to analyses. First, while the Quran does recognize Jesus as the Prophet of God and Messiah, it seems the knowledge of the writer about him is somewhat "different." While the Quran says he was born of a virgin, Miriam, it also says she is the sister of Harun (Aaron). The only Miriam in the bible that had a brother named Aaron was Miriam, the sister of Moses. Could an Oral tradition about Jesus been handed down to the compilers of the Quran, thereby having a mix-up of stories concerning his life?

Now, the Quran also refers to a figure known as "The Mahdi" who will come to rule the Muslims in Righteousness and oppose the Anti-Christ called Dajjal. This Mahdi's army would ultimately be saved from destruction by the miraculous appearance of Jesus Christ. Jesus will help him defeat the enemies of Islam and bring a reign of peace on earth for a period. After some time, a group of unstoppable beings will revolt against the Mahdi and kill him. Jesus will take vengeance on these super beings and destroy them. After this, Jesus himself will rule the world forever. I felt it necessary to point out what we understand to be the fundamental eschatological beliefs of Islam are as it relates to Jesus Christ and the end of time. Unfortunately, most Muslims do not know what the Quran teaches about Christ.

IN SEARCH OF THE KINGDOM

The Catholic church was part of the Orthodox Church until the schism that separated them both in 1054. The organization founded by Emperor Constantine in the early 4th Century was an attempt to bring the disparate nationalities of the Roman empire together under one religion. The leaders of the other two monotheistic religions: the Arabs and the Khazars used the same system. The Khazars adopted Judaism as its State religion.

The Catholic and Eastern Orthodox churches are unique. They have served as a repository of the historical evolution of world religion, beginning from the very earliest African religions through the Babylonian era, and to this time. In their rituals and practices, they express rites and ceremonies that were performed long before the birth of Christ. For example, the doctrinal belief of the Immaculate Conception of the Catholic/ Orthodox comes from the Egyptian myth about the goddess Asat (sometimes referred to as Isis). The church declared Mary, Jesus' mother, to be born without sin, thereby ascribing to her the privilege of an Immaculate Birth. The Egyptians held the same doctrine concerning Aset/Isis, the mother of Heru/Horus.

Concerning Aset, the story goes that her husband Asar/Osiris was killed by his brother Set, who scattered his body parts into the river Nile river. Aset was able to recover all except his penis. She reassembled all of what she could find, thirteen in all, but made a replica of the missing part from wood. It was his Penis. Aset conceived a son she named Heru by following divine instructions regarding what to do so that Asar could impregnate her through the wooden penis (see Figure 9).

*Figure 9 – Bronze statue of Isis nursing Horus, Egypt,
600-30 BCE. Science Museum London.*

This Heru would go on to avenge his father's death by neutralizing the power of his uncle Set with the help of the god Amun-Re. In the bible, Jesus is referred to as the Amen in the book of Revelation. (We get the word "Amen" from the name of this god. We also get our word Sunray from this Egyptian god, and the word for Sunset from Assar's brother Set, who killed him). So, every evening when the sun goes down, we say it is "Sun Set" or Set has killed the Sun. There are much symbolism and allegory in these Egyptian characters that we would have to write a whole book to show their relationship to all the three monotheistic religions.

Next, we look at the origins of Judaism. It is vital to make a distinction between Judaism and the Hebrew faith practiced by Jesus and the early biblical prophets. Judaism is a more recent phenomenon and religion. The Roman general, Vespasian, led the destruction of the city of Jerusalem in 70 A.D. and later became Emperor of Rome. Yohannan Ben Zakkai became friends with Vespasian during the rebellion that led to the destruction of Jerusalem. When Vespasian became the Emperor, a group of prominent Judaic scholars led by Zakkai, obtained permission to establish a new brand of the Judaic religion more palatable to the Roman Empire.

It is significant to point out that the Hebrew faith had begun to undergo an enormous change at least five centuries before the destruction of Jerusalem. For example, most of the Israelites during the time of Jesus spoke Aramaic and not Hebrew. The corrupted Levitical Priesthood was now staffed by those who showed allegiance to Herod and the Kings, and who submitted to Rome's authority. The Talmud mentions Yohannan Ben Zakkai was the person that convinced the Jews that they did not have to reestablish the animal sacrifice in Jerusalem. Zakkai's rationale was God had said through his prophets, *"I prefer obedience rather than sacrifice"* (Hos. 6:6).

The previous discussion demonstrates that Judaism is surprisingly younger than the Christian faith. The period during which the Israelites of the bible were taken into captivity, around 400 BC in Babylon, signaled the end of biblical Hebraic belief. By the time of Jesus, a new religious system had begun to take shape, which is the progenitor of today's Judaism. Even during Jesus' time, the Temple had more than one High Priest at a time due to the conflict between the Pharisees and Sadducees over doctrine. *"Annas and Caiaphas being the high priests, the word of God came unto John the son of Zacharias in the wilderness.* "(Lk. 3:2).

Judaism, as we know it, began in the late 1st and early 2nd Century CE thanks to the effort of Ben Zakkai. The practices of Judaism today are also influenced mostly by Babylonian and Persian traditions whose origin is of somewhat opaque sources. The specific birth of Judaism as we know it today occurred shortly after the destruction of the Jerusalem Temple and the absorption of some loyal Jews by the Romans. The Romans permitted the Jews to initiate "schools" that would teach a new non-Jerusalem focused theology. The Rabbis who headed these schools were the originators of Modern Judaism and the initial authors of the Mishna and Talmud, the real Judaic Holy Books. As I stated earlier, the primary Rabbi of this era was *Johanan Ben Zakkai*. He can be called the father of Judaism (*Neusner, J. 1970*). Some of the practices that remain which are biblical include circumcision of males, avoidance of pork, and observance of Sabbaths. However, these are practices found among many other peoples who have no claim of biblical origin. It seems the Talmuds (Babylonian and Palestinian) would offer more clarity on the origins of Judaism. One other significant source of influence was the conversion of the Khaganates of Khazaria in South-Central Europe around the 9th century. This mass conversion gave new life to the waning number of practicing Jews in Europe and Asia. Today, over 80% of people who identify with the religion descended from the Khazars.

Some of the unique facets of Judaism that make it distinct from biblical Hebrew traditions are the matrilineal descent of its adherents and doctrinal supremacy of the Talmud. The Talmud was unknown during the time of the Apostolic and pre-Christian era. While there are Judaic who hold the Torah and Tanakh to be superior to the Talmud, the Talmud IS the book of Faith for guidance used by most. Finally, Hebrew prophets surely wrote the Hebrew scriptures before the exilic period, and if written in Hebrew, would have been written using the Paleo-Hebrew script. However, there are as yet no known fragments of scripture found in the Paleo-Hebrew writing system. While I am convinced that it was in use as early as the 10th century BC, this writing form was lost to the post-exilic Judaic and gentiles until much recently deciphered. Even today, most people believe that the so-called "wailing wall" is a remnant of the old Solomonic Temple. The "wailing wall" is the remnant of a Roman Barracks. Jesus had stated that not one stone of the Temple would be left standing:

> *And as he went out of the temple, one of his disciples saith unto him, Master, see what manner of stones and what buildings are here! And Jesus answering said unto him, Seest thou these great buildings? <u>there shall not be left one stone upon another</u>, that shall not be thrown down (Mk.13:1-2).*

The expectation of a Messiah has been the subtle undertone of almost all known religions. The Hindu Messiah, Krishna, has many similarities to the description of

Jesus Christ. Including the facts that his real Father was God, his earthly father was a Carpenter, and Wise Men who followed a Star heralded their births. Ruling Kings (Krishna's Uncle, Kamsa) committed infanticide. In an attempt to scuttle their advent, both cast out demons and were raised from the dead, (Vanamali, D.2012).

Now when most people hear this, the usual reaction is to assume someone copied from some script and is putting together a well-designed fable. However, if you read the gospels, you will find out that the writers recorded many seemingly insignificant things Jesus did as fulfilling some "scripture" or another. The problem lies with our contemporary orientation into believing that such prophecy could not have been given to other people outside Israel BEFORE Jesus was born on earth as THE MESSIAH. Our previous example concerning Balaam is evidence that non-Israelites received messages from God. Isaiah and other Old Testament prophets often referred to the future acts of Jesus in the Past-Tense. For example, Isaiah 53 it says:

> *He is despised and rejected of men; a man of sorrows and acquainted with grief: and we hid as it were our faces from him; he was despised, and we esteemed him not. Surely, he hath borne our griefs, and carried our sorrows: yet we did esteem him stricken, smitten of God, and afflicted. But he was wounded for our transgressions, he was bruised for our iniquities: the chastisement of our peace was upon him; and with his stripes we are healed. All we like sheep have gone astray; we have turned every one to his own way; and the LORD hath laid on him the iniquity of us all. He was oppressed, and he was afflicted, yet he opened not his mouth: he is brought as a lamb to the slaughter, and as a sheep before her shearers is dumb, so he openeth not his mouth. He was taken from prison and from judgment: and who shall declare his generation? for he was cut off out of the land of the living: for the transgression of my people was he stricken (Is. 53:3-8).*

Most biblical scholars assume even the book of Job, the oldest known scripture, to be about a man who existed before Israel existed. The bible refers to Jethro, the father in law of Moses, as the Priest of Median, who knew God.

Now the account we read earlier about Heru, Asar, and Aset is like the story of a Risen savior. Heru is born supernaturally through Asat but is the Son of Asar. He goes into a desert to combat Set the enemy that killed his father. He raises the dead and performs other miracles. However, we need to be clear on an important point. The Egyptians had many thousands of years of history and most likely edited their beliefs over time. It should not be surprising if now and then we find similarities between their Heroes and Christ. Secondly, a lot of 19th-century pseudo mystics muddled anthropological research with lies about similarities between Jesus and Heru.

The so-called "Christian Holidays" are astronomical observations correlating to what the ancients believed about the trajectory of the celestial bodies. For example, Christmas symbolized the period in which the Sun reached its lowest ebb between late December and early January. For that reason, we see that the Eastern Orthodox churches and the Western Catholic churches have different dates for the observance of Christmas. The Eastern holding on to the older tradition.

The same is true of Easter. It symbolized a time of Spring and the return of the Sun. It is no coincidence that the time of Christmas is roughly Nine months from the time of Spring. So, the "baby" is born in December, Nine months after springtime, with its fertility rites. Some examples of the fertility rites during the spring (Easter) are: searching for eggs, eating only fish on good Friday, cuddling Easter bunnies, and other practices that symbolize fertility. The Western Church maintained the tradition of alternating the Easter day based on the planetary movements of the celestial bodies, even though it chooses a permanent day for Christmas.

In the Ifa religion and other variants of African spirituality, the sacrifice of goats, bulls, birds, and sometimes humans, expresses the concept of a redeemer to serve as a propitiation for sins and spells. We cannot overemphasize the significance of these rituals because they foreshadow the ultimate sacrifice made to make unnecessary all other blood sacrifices in the time to come.

SOCIETY AND FAITH

SOCIETIES DEVELOP MORAL CONSTRUCTS OF WRONG AND RIGHT based on several factors unique to their peoples. Often communities create a culture of pillaging to meet the needs of its people due to the barren and harsh agricultural terrain it inhabits. The fact that this stealing and murdering is evil would not deter the inhabitants or its leadership from continuing in such seemingly immoral behavior. When a society has dwelt in such conditions for hundreds, or perhaps thousands of years, a certain kind of cognitive dissonance develops that serves as a shield of justification for such barbarism.

Even today, the difference between the moral values of the "Christian" nations and the formerly "savage" peoples of Africa and the Americas are evident. Societies advanced in science and knowledge left a legacy of barbarism and murder now inherited by once peaceful "savages." It is a little-known fact that in Pre-Colonial Africa, for example, there were no prisons. The crime rate did not warrant any such institution. Children were rarely born out of wedlock. Honesty in business was so normative that apparently, traders would leave their products out for sale with pebbles indicating how many cowries the passerby needed to deposit before picking up the merchandise. At the end of the day, the trader collected the remainder of her wares and money. This way, she could both earn an income and be a Homemaker. With the advent of the Arab and European conquests, these values seem to have disappeared. Not because of these religions that came with those cultures; but because of the cultures that brought these religions.

Historically, the Hellenistic cultures had little moral scruples about the unnatural sexual relationship between persons of the same sex, or between Adult males and boys. This culture spread with the conquering advance of the Grecian Armies that conquered the Mediterranean, North Africa, the Levant, and parts of Asia. Currently, this moral problem is prevalent in these parts and in institutions like the Roman Church that has spread this culture of the Greeks. Today, deviant behavior that was unheard of in other parts of the world has been introduced to unwilling cultures by the force of economic and political necessity.

The social impact of these deviant behaviors, now normalized, immunizes the effect of Faith in the lives of people. All over the world, today, moral decadence is acceptable because some of the worst deviations are now government-sanctioned. How can a child, whose family taught her that Stealing and Homosexuality are sins, choose informedly if the Government convinces her that Homosexuality is not a sin? If all cultures for thousands of years taught both homosexuality and stealing are sins, then if one was okay all this time, why would the other not be also?

One of the greatest myths perpetuated by society on both young and old is about the value of the modern educational system. The contemporary education system is like no other institution created by man to deceive and to destroy the morals of the young. On the surface, it sounds like a good deal. Leave your children with the government and go about your business. The government will "educate" them for you. The truth is more and more children are going to elementary and secondary schools as little angels but returning to their parents as little devils. Their value systems become warped, and they become enemies of all that their parents and background held sacred. It is like a subtle form of the Chinese "Cultural Revolution" of Chairman Mao.

The intent of the modern school system, established in the mid-19th century, was to develop a class of people who would be dependent on others for the provision of their sustenance. If you speak with an average student today, you will discover that her intention and those of her parent is that she graduates and "finds a good job." The system takes the dream of productivity and bringing something new into the world from a child upon entry into the elementary school system. Statistics indicate the bonds between parent and child, are replaced by those between the child and her peers when she attends primary school. The child is "schooled" to be obedient to hierarchy, and robbed of her God-given inquisitiveness. For those with a stronger Will to be free, their actions are considered rebellious by the school "system." The child may begin her journey into the "Justice System" if the adults are not vigilant and protective.

Furthermore, after a child spends four years in the university, she often will not find a job in the field for which she has trained, rendering the whole purpose useless. In rare instances, these children find themselves practicing the field they studied in school. The exceptions are often in the areas of Law, Medicine, and Engineering. These exceptions might exist because the practitioners of these professions command the most financial resources and can influence governments to limit the number of persons that can enter those fields of study. Does it make sense for a person to spend seven years just to be able to diagnose a fever, or conduct medical General Practice? Undoubtedly, more complicated therapeutic areas such as Brain surgery call for more intense study.

This new society distorted the relationships between men and women. Modernity systematically dissolved the fundamental role of mothers as nurturers, and fathers as protectors for what is today called "modern." It is taboo to use the term "housewife," even though that is what the agreement in a marriage connotes. In the marriage contract, a woman will take the name of a man, and then live with him forever, taking care of his home and all that pertains to it. Defining marriage in this traditional manner is a taboo even for those who claim to be people of Faith.

Today society expects a woman to carry half of the economic responsibility of the home, as well as nurture the children. For the few with the financial resources, this is a workable situation, but for most people, it is impossible. For this reason, the pursuit of the untenable relationship foisted upon them by popular culture and modernity, strains the marriage relationships.

The children are the great victims of this pursuit of conformity by the parents. All studies indicate children experience a more wholesome development when raised by their mothers and fathers rather than by strangers and institutions. Nevertheless, mothers are ashamed to raise their young children and tend their homes as housewives. The fathers are also threatened by a system that sees them as an obstacle to the reengineering of society. Most men in the "advanced" societies live in quiet fear of their wives. They know that they have a rival for the loyalty of their wives, *the Welfare State*. When a woman requests a divorce, *the Welfare State* takes the role of the husband. The government immediately provides her all she needs; often on the condition, she has little children to offer up to the State welfare system. Unknown to most people, there is a terrible price to pay—an amount paid by their children in the long run.

People must begin to conduct marriages without State or Government Marriage Certificates, which might sound revolutionary, but it is not. The dangers to society of government authorized marriages will need a whole book of its own to describe. Some of the unforeseen hazards of Court or Government marriages are: that it gives Judges, who usually have no personal relationship with any of the spouses the power to determine what and how properties should be shared, assess the needs of the children, and impose sanctions on married couples who find themselves in Divorce Courts. Giving couples the option to return to their religious or traditional institutions, who have a stake in seeing them succeed, would diminish our divorce and child trauma rates. The Legal system is not an appropriate place for the settlement of family disputes because it is an adversarial system. In marriage and family disputes, there are no winners, only losers. The worst losers are children who must suffer the heart-wrenching trauma of seemingly helpless adults. Secular laws should never govern marriage. If there is a need to guarantee the future financial well-being of spouses, then Legal, Non-Marriage contracts can be Signed relating to Property. We are not referring to Prenups. Those are also part of the Legal system. The Bible has advised us in the book of 1ˢᵗ Corinthians:

> *Dare any of you, having a matter against another, go to law before the unjust, and not before the saints? Do ye not know that the saints shall judge the world? and if the world shall be judged by you, are ye unworthy to judge the smallest matters? Know ye not that we shall judge angels? how much more things that pertain to this life? If then ye have judgments of things pertaining to this life, set them to judge who are least esteemed in the church. I speak to your shame. Is it so, that there is not a wise man among you? no, not one that shall be able to judge between his brethren? But brother goeth to law with brother, and that before the unbelievers. Now therefore there is utterly a fault among you, because ye go to law one with another. Why do ye not rather take wrong? why do ye not rather suffer yourselves to be defrauded? Nay, ye do wrong, and defraud, and that your brethren (I Cor. 6:1-8).*

The more people become dependent on the State, the less they can assert their God-given Rights and responsibilities on matters that concern their children. Schools tell quiet boys and boisterous girls that they are "Gay." Movie and Pop Stars are used as agents to sell these philosophies to children. The system tags the father or mother that opposes such blasphemous propositions as anti-social, and a bigot. Resistance and confrontation can reverse this moral plague infecting the world.

If society were amenable to the teachings of Christ and his Apostles, we would have a much better and harmonious world. The teachings of Jesus and his apostles stress the respect for traditions and cultures of all societies as long as they do not infringe on clearly stated Commandments of God. They teach that the believers must make prayers, supplications, and thanksgiving to God on behalf of the Kings, Presidents, and Emperors of the lands in which they sojourn:

> *I exhort therefore, that, first of all, supplications, prayers, intercessions, and giving of thanks, be made for all men; For kings, and for all that are in authority; that we may lead a quiet and peaceable life in all godliness and honesty. For this is good and acceptable in the sight of God our Saviour (1 Tim. 2:1-3).*

It does not pit classes of society against each other, and it exposes the unreasonableness of Racism. *"Then answered the Jews, and said unto him, Say we not well that thou art a Samaritan, and hast a devil? Jesus answered, I have not a devil; but I honour my Father, and ye do dishonour me"* (Jn. 8:48-49). In this passage, Jesus is insulted by the Judaic by saying he has a devil and is a Samaritan (calling a person a Samaritan in those days was worse than calling him a Devil). However, Jesus never denied being a Samaritan. He simply responded by saying he was not a Devil. So, from Jesus' example, we see that he did not consider one group of people better than another simply based on ethnicity. Any Christian who practices the opposite is either not one or is immature.

ECONOMICS AND FAITH

A CCORDING TO THE BIBLE, MONEY IS NECESSARY TO ACCOMPLISH most objectives in life: *"A feast is made for laughter, and wine maketh merry: but money answereth all things"* (Eccl. 10:19). It also says that the Love of money is the root of all evil. *"For the love of money is the root of all evil: which while some coveted after, they have erred from the faith, and pierced themselves through with many sorrows "*(1 Tim. 6:10). It is important from the onset to state that the present economic world system is completely unbiblical and contrary to the scriptural teaching on basic economics. Yes, there is such a thing as biblical economics. One of the most fundamental differences between God's economic theory and that which we operate today is the system of money lending. Today, just like in the time of Jesus, when he drove the money changers out of the Temple, believers think it is normal to borrow and lend at interest. The following bible verses make it clear where God's heart is on this issue. *"If thou lend money to any of my people that is poor by thee, thou shalt not be to him as an usurer, neither shalt thou lay upon him usury"* (Ex. 22:25).

> *LORD, who shall abide in thy tabernacle? who shall dwell in thy holy hill? He that walketh uprightly, and worketh righteousness, and speaketh the truth in his heart. He that backbiteth not with his tongue, nor doeth evil to his neighbour, nor taketh up a reproach against his neighbour. In whose eyes a vile person is contemned; but he honoureth them that fear the LORD. He that sweareth to his own hurt, and changeth not. He that putteth not out his money to usury, nor taketh reward against the innocent. He that doeth these things shall never be moved (Ps. 15:1-5).*

Evil culture and tendencies seem to dominate the world because most people wake up each day to pursue some form of gain, primarily financial gain. It does not matter what religion dominates an area of the world; the primary aim of each person is how to acquire more and more. The pursuit of more is no less a vice for the poor, as it is for the rich. We wake up each day seeking money before seeking God. Therefore, it is necessary to discuss the creation of wealth and how to pursue it in harmony with the Will of God. Lack of understanding of how has led many astray and affected the reputation of the gospel.

For this reason, we ought to understand a little bit about money, and why it seems to have such a hold on humankind. After all, money in and of itself is an inanimate object. It cannot have any value except that thrust upon it by the same people who worship it. Without their worship, it is of no significance. So, we need to understand Economics as a science, especially the part of it that deals with Finance. We must understand what impact the normalization of "Usury" has had on all the people of the world today. The consistent diminishing of the value of money because of Interest-based lending, rather than profit participatory lending. In profit participatory lending, the lender shares in the profit or loss of the borrower.

Economics is the science of allocating Scarce resources across high demand. Simply put, we "economize" to make our resources go as far as possible in meeting our needs. Three critical elements interact with each other to produce a surplus beyond our needs. The factors of Production are Land, Labor, and Capital. This surplus is what you would call wealth. Money is the measure of wealth. So, money is a measuring instrument of the operations of the three factors of Production. Money itself is not Capital. It is merely a medium of exchange for either Land, Labor, or Capital. An example of Capital is an industrial machine or a wheelbarrow when deployed toward Production.

According to the scriptures, a person who has unusual "Skill" in his career will sit with Kings, and not ordinary people. "*Seest thou a man diligent in his business? he shall stand before kings; he shall not stand before mean men*" (Prov. 22:29). So, it is evident from a scriptural perspective that engaging <u>skillfully</u> in the Production of Goods or Services increases the probability of obtaining great wealth. To create wealth in any society, the leadership must work continually on increasing the skill set of its citizens in the individual's choice of economic activity.

Secondly, wealth is something that is created by humans with help from above, and not necessarily something that appears without productive effort: "*But thou shalt remember the LORD thy God: for it is he that giveth thee power to get wealth, that he may establish his covenant which he sware unto thy fathers, as it is this day*" (Deut. 8:18). Work requires work. However, today many people believe that merely praying and not working can change their financial destiny. No doubt, prayer removes obstacles that distort our progress toward wealth creation. However, prayer alone will not make us financially successful. It is not for nothing that the scriptures say that if a person will not work, let him not eat:

For even when we were with you, this we commanded you, that if any would not work, neither should he eat. For we hear that there are some which walk among you disorderly, working not at all, but are busybodies. Now them that are such we command and exhort by our Lord Jesus Christ, that with quietness they work, and eat their own bread. But ye, brethren, be not weary in well doing (2 Thess. 3:10).

Learning to keep our minds on the things pleasing to God will not hinder us from being financially prosperous or providing for our families. However, we must be willing to forsake great wealth if it will distract us from the Lord for one day:

For after all these things do the Gentiles seek: for your heavenly Father knoweth that ye have need of all these things. But seek ye first the kingdom of God, and his righteousness; and all these things shall be added unto you (Matt. 6:32-33).

In our pursuit of financial success or pleasure, we should please the Lord. As much as possible, the choices you make in your pursuit of happiness should not make another person despise or doubt the efficacy of God's work in your life.

The sum of what we have said so far about money is that it is a representative of the surplus of our productive capacity called wealth. For example, if I make shoes, I will not make shoes to put on every person's feet before mine. I will make a shoe for myself first rather than buy from a competitor. The extra shoes I make are those I would take to the market to sell. These extra shoes are my wealth (Surplus).

Of course, carrying them about is bulky, so I must find some way of proving to those I want to buy shirts or food from that I have shoes that are of equal or greater value to that which I want from them. The way I do this is by tendering a Certificate, acceptable to them, that proves that I do have a surplus of shoes. This certificate of wealth is called Money. The "certificate" may or may not be credit.

This certificate is often issued by a Third Party who is Chartered by society to act as an independent auditor of financial transactions. We often call that Government, Banks, or as Jesus once said, Caesar. Problems arise when this independent entity begins to write certificates for goods that don't exist or begins to award certificates to those who are not legitimate owners of the documents. Over time it results in inefficiencies and poverty in a society. So, you can see naturally rich countries with talented people and natural resources gasping for food and water. All this is because the government or Banks have disregarded the scripture found in the book of Proverbs. *"A false balance is abomination to the LORD: but a just weight is his delight"* (Prov. 11:1). When big businesses that donate to politicians are about to fail and go the natural way of failure, the governments work to protect them by giving them public money to stay afloat. They never do the same for the small family running a small business. They justify this wickedness by claiming that the big companies are "systemically significant." The Lord sees this hypocrisy. He will require it from those that perpetuate this evil. If a business is no longer serving the natural value chain, it should be allowed to follow the path of nature. When we show favoritism for the firms that control society, we bring a worse condition on all people eventually.

When these things begin to happen, and financial hardship becomes intolerable, many people start turning to the superstitious or criminal activities to meet their needs. An understanding of what scripture says about Economics, and a willingness to trust the Lord's guidance will see you through. Do not get carried away with superstitious doctrines and a desire for wicked short cuts. You ought to know that the scriptures state that if you are diligent in your work, you will sit with Kings and not with average men. You should sharpen your skills in your line of work as well as understand the economic and political environment in which you are operating. I cannot reiterate enough that Paul's appreciation of the socio-economic and political situation of his environment provided the context for most of his commands concerning money. It is biblical to continually upgrade your knowledge, skills, and abilities *"Through desire a man, having separated himself, seeketh and intermeddleth with all wisdom"* (Prov. 18:1). You should partner with others of like-mind to start a business because the bible teaches that there is strength in numbers for human activities:

> *Two are better than one, because they have a good reward for their labour. For if they fall, the one will lift up his fellow: but woe to him that is alone when he falleth; for he hath not another to help him up. Again, if two lie together, then they have heat: but how can one be warm alone? And if one prevail against him, two shall withstand him; and a threefold cord is not quickly broken (Eccl. 4:9-12).*

A *liberal* economy, a *command* economy, or some mix of both provide the basis for managing society. You ought to know under what kind of economy you are operating. Is it one in which the ability to establish a business is simple and not cumbersome? Are you able to keep more of the profits you make rather than hand it over as Taxes to some people from the Tax collector's office? Then you are operating under a liberal economic system. Are undue burdens placed on you as to what you should produce or how much?

Does the government engage in businesses that Private individuals can perform? If your answer is yes, then you are operating under a Command economic system, and it will be more difficult to develop economically in that environment. Under a liberal economy, there is more opportunity for Private wealth creation, and people are free to pursue their visions while meeting the **Demand** of their customers.

Some common sense understanding of economics will help a person avoid the pitfalls of religious charlatans. They obtain money from the gullible and straightforward believer in money-making spells. I do not doubt the overruling power of God to miraculously provide material goods for sincere believers as Jesus did when fcd the 5000, "not including women and children." However, he never demanded upfront money for his miraculous provisions.

> *And when it was evening, his disciples came to him, saying, This is a desert place, and the time is now past; send the multitude away, that they may go into the villages, and buy themselves victuals. But Jesus said unto them, They need not depart; give ye them to eat. And they say unto him, We have here but five loaves, and two fishes. He said, Bring them hither to me. And he commanded the multitude to sit down on the grass, and took the five loaves, and the two fishes, and looking up to heaven, he blessed, and brake, and gave the loaves to his disciples, and the disciples to the multitude. And they did all eat, and were filled: and they took up of the fragments that remained twelve baskets full. And they that had eaten were about five thousand men, beside women and children (Matt. 14:15-21).*

God has given man a Free Will. Therefore, we should follow his example by allowing people to pursue their passions without the hindrance of State or Government. So long as that freedom does not impact the safety and wellbeing of others. Indeed, adults *ought* to exercise their freedoms within the framework of respecting the conscience and feelings of other adults. It is in this freedom of activities and exchange that a balance and equilibrium can be obtained and managed until the "Coming of the Lord" when wc shall know and understand better. *"All things are lawful for me, but all things are not expedient: all things are lawful for me, but all things edify not. Let no man seek his own, but every man another's wealth"* (1 Corinthians 10:23-24).

We should not become lazy and use the gospel of God as a means of money-making. Jesus overturning of the tables in wrath was related to the practice of merchandising the articles of faith and religion. God rejected the concept of making a profit by merely lending money in the old testament. Still, in the gospels, we see that it was such a prevalent practice that it was happening in the Temples and synagogues. While the gospel of Christ, unlike Moses, does not state "do not lend money with interest," the gospels suggest that it was a practice that did not please Jesus.

Now, with the rate of inflation worldwide, and economic hardship seemingly inescapable, society needs to look again at what the bible teaches about "usury." Though the teachings of Jesus are not mechanical, we advise that lenders should split the risk of loss, and the possibility of gain, between both the lender and the borrower. If the lender feels the purpose of the borrower has the potential of profit, he should lend. If he doubts the viability of the venture, he should not provide funds. His Yes should be yes, and his No should be no. It is no surprise that our current banking and lending system turned the whole earth into economic slaves: *"The rich ruleth over the poor, and the borrower is servant to the lender"* (Prov. 22:7). You cannot be sure that any enterprise you enter in will be successful exactly when you planned for it to be. For this reason, borrowing with the promise to pay back is a dangerous proposal that is not encouraged by Christ: *"But let your communication be, Yea, yea; Nay, nay: for whatsoever is more than these cometh of evil. "*(Matt. 5:37).

The insatiability of man's desires has been the fundamental basis of all the evil in the earth. The object of this desire becomes a sort of god to man. Since the invention of money as the primary "Medium of Exchange" for Goods and Services, it has become the most potent force, second only to the power of God in the lives of men. The absolute dependence on economic theories and the temporal value of money causes a condition the Bible refers to as "adultery." Biblical adultery is the situation in which a person professes to be committed to God. Yet, all her heart's desire is for more Goods. The money becomes a source for all that her heart desires, pushing God into the background. She begins to attempt to serve "two masters" but cannot. Eventually, she must choose between one or the other. *"No man can serve two masters: for either he will hate the one, and love the other; or else he will hold to the one, and despise the other. Ye cannot serve God and mammon "*(Matt. 6:24).

God knows that we require money. However, he wants it to be OUR servant and not the other way around. He is not pleased when he sees the awe and fear we display towards material things that glitter. The fact is, based on scripture; God wants you to be as financially wealthy as you can handle. The fact that Jesus lived a sparse life did not mean he was poor. He always was able to provide for what he needed. Part of the purpose of his death and resurrection was to give us the ability to be financially successful in this life. However, financial success is a means to an end and not an end in and of itself. *"For ye know the grace of our Lord Jesus Christ, that, though he was rich, yet for your sakes he became poor, that ye through his poverty might be rich "*(2 Cor. 8:9) *"Ye lust, and have not: ye kill, and desire to have, and cannot obtain: ye fight and war, yet ye have not, because ye ask not. Ye ask, and receive not, because ye ask amiss, that ye may consume it upon your lusts"* (Jas. 4:2-3). *"But seek ye first the kingdom of God, and his righteousness; and all these things shall be added unto you"* (Matt. 6:33).

MATERIAL SECURITY FROM A PURPOSE FILLED LIFE

THIS BOOK CONCENTRATES ON THE THEOLOGICAL AND eschatological nature of the understanding of Christ, beginning with this chapter. First, I will start with a cursory look at the nature of man and our need for physical and metaphysical security.

The pursuit of material things is a character trait found in all living creatures: all others for Need, but man mostly for Want, and Lust. It is the aspect of our nature that leads to insecurity and lust. If an individual has the basic needs of food and shelter, she is expected by God to be content. You can find even the most terrifying animal to be meek and playful if it has eaten enough for its need, but a human's Want seems to be insatiable. She continues to crave more and more and is never satisfied. This nature of man is both good and bad. It is good because it is what makes us eternal and always in pursuit of knowing God. It could be bad because, in this life, it can cause us to lose sight of whom we should be pursuing and lead us to pursue illusory things. This misdirection of our desires leads us down the path of eternal dissatisfaction, also referred to as *Hell:*

> *There was a certain rich man, which was clothed in purple and fine linen, and fared sumptuously every day: And there was a certain beggar named Lazarus, which was laid at his gate, full of sores, And desiring to be fed with the crumbs which fell from the rich man's table: moreover the dogs came and licked his sores. And it came to pass, that the beggar died, and was carried by the angels into Abraham's bosom: the rich man also died, and was buried; And in hell he lift up his eyes, being in torments, and seeth Abraham afar off, and Lazarus in his bosom. And he cried and said, Father Abraham, have mercy on me, and send Lazarus, <u>that he may dip the tip of his finger in water, and cool my tongue; for I am tormented in this flame</u>. But Abraham said, Son, remember that thou in thy lifetime receivedst thy good things, and likewise Lazarus evil things: but now he is comforted, and*

thou art tormented. And beside all this, between us and you there is a great gulf fixed: so that they which would pass from hence to you cannot; neither can they pass to us, that would come from thence. Then he said, I pray thee therefore, father, that thou wouldest send him to my father's house: For I have five brethren; that he may testify unto them, lest they also come into this place of torment. Abraham saith unto him, They have Moses and the prophets; let them hear them (Luke 16:19-29).

Please note that the "Fire" was IN him, not around him. The pursuit of material things can lead to Hell, a place of perpetual want and perpetual lack. The man did not go to hell because he was rich. He went there because he was so attached to material things that, even when the man had more than enough, the man was so greedy and self-centered that he could not spare a little for the starving Lazarus.

The grand pursuit of the Soul is *Rest*. When we pursue romantic Love, wealth, fame, etc. what we are doing is seeking Rest. Rest does not mean inactivity or inertia. It implies a sense of security and satisfaction. However, Rest comes when we find PEACE WITH GOD. When we seek to find this rest in any other thing, we could become frustrated and disillusioned, and soon blame others for our spiritual condition. There is a pursuit of wealth that leads to dissatisfaction and possible hatred of kin and even infidelity in marriages.

After God, we also seek to find rest in people. We want to have a person of the opposite sex who can be a comforter of sorts. It is the same for women and men. For women, there is a need to be loved, while for men, the need to be respected is primary, but he also desires to have a woman that replaces his mother in emotional care. This desire seems like a contradiction in men, but it is true. If we use material things as a measure of the degree to which our spouses or lovers are expressing these sentiments to us, we may end up pursuing these material things to the detriment of our relationships with people. For those whose pursuit is wealth, they set their relationship towards a possible shipwreck.

Understanding what the purpose of life is can be liberating to those who seek after rest. It is easier to begin to understand the general principles of the objectives of life than to understand what the purpose of your personal life is. I find a lot of people want to know what the purpose of *their* life is when they do not even know what the general goal of life is. Often a person will say I wish I knew what the Will of God is concerning this or that. However, I think that such quests are a bit like putting the horse before the proverbial cart.

First, ask, "what is the purpose of life." Once you begin to understand that, then you can start to ask questions about details such as "what is the purpose of MY life?" The purpose of life is to know God and to know him as Jesus Christ (John 17:3). To know Him is to become like Christ; to become like him, you must traverse some discomforts and hardships. During this process, you must be in a mode of self-control and continue without bitterness towards God, people, or circumstances. Achieving this is not something that you can accomplish without the Grace of God himself through his person of Jesus Christ.

Your greatest enemy in knowing the purpose of life is your human effort in obeying the Law of God. Does this sound strange? Well, almost everything the Apostle Paul wrote about was about how the Law was the chief cause of our separation from God. Every creature just acts itself, but we are continually trying to be something we are not. Our human constitution is distant from that which the Law of God demands. Rather than acknowledge the futility of attaining its requirements, we continue to strive for the perfection required by the Law. This contradiction within ourselves demonstrates to us that we are functioning at cross purposes to that which comes naturally with us. We need to appreciate that only by the power of the presence of Christ, can we slowly be transformed into that which God expects from us.

The bible says the Law itself is a good thing but that it causes you to die when you allow it to dictate your relationship with God:

> What shall we say then? Is the law sin? God forbid. Nay, I had not known sin, but by the law: for I had not known lust, except the law had said, Thou shalt not covet. But sin, taking occasion by the commandment, wrought in me all manner of concupiscence. For without the law sin was dead. For I was alive without the law once: but when the commandment came, sin revived, and I died. And the commandment, which was ordained to life, I found to be unto death. For sin, taking occasion by the commandment, deceived me, and by it slew me. Wherefore the law is holy, and the commandment holy, and just, and good. Was then that which is good made death unto me? God forbid. But sin, that it might appear sin, working death in me by that which is good; that sin by the commandment might become exceeding sinful. For we know that the law is spiritual: but I am carnal, sold under sin. For that which I do I allow not: for what I would, that do I not; but what I hate, that do I. If then I do that which I would not, I consent unto the law that it is good. Now then it is no more I that do it, but sin that dwelleth in me. For I know that in me (that is, in my flesh,) dwelleth no good thing: for to will is present with me; but how to

perform that which is good I find not. For the good that I would I do not: but the evil which I would not, that I do. Now if I do that I would not, it is no more I that do it, but sin that dwelleth in me. I find then a law, that, when I would do good, evil is present with me. For I delight in the law of God after the inward man: But I see another law in my members, warring against the law of my mind, and bringing me into captivity to the law of sin which is in my members (Rom. 7:7-23).

To die in this passage means to be separated from God. Separation from God is a particularly important part of this book. You must take the time to understand what I have just said. It is critical to understand the rest of the book. Had the rich man whom we read about known, he would have confessed to God that he had a problem and asked God to deliver him from the bondage of self-centeredness. God would have helped him out of obligation. He just never asked for help, nor recognized a need for it.

It is often perplexing to discover how seeking to find peace with God by observing the Laws of God is considered a sin by the scriptures:

For the law having a shadow of good things to come, and not the very image of the things, can never with those sacrifices which they offered year by year continually make the comers thereunto perfect. For then would they not have ceased to be offered? because that the worshippers once purged should have had no more conscience of sins. But in those sacrifices there is a remembrance again made of sins every year. For it is not possible that the blood of bulls and of goats should take away sins. Wherefore when he cometh into the world, he saith, Sacrifice and offering thou wouldest not, but a body hast thou prepared me: In burnt offerings and sacrifices for sin thou hast had no pleasure. Then said I, Lo, I come (in the volume of the book it is written of me,) to do thy will, O God. Above when he said, Sacrifice and offering and burnt offerings and offering for sin thou wouldest not, neither hadst pleasure therein; which are offered by the law; Then said he, Lo, I come to do thy will, O God. He taketh away the first, that he may establish the second. By the which will we are sanctified through the offering of the body of Jesus Christ once for all (Heb.10:1-10).

Also, in the following verses, he warns against substituting simple faith in Christ with obedience to the Laws:

For if we sin wilfully after that, we have received the knowledge of the truth, there remaineth no more sacrifice for sins, But a certain fearful looking for of judgment and fiery indignation, which shall devour the adversaries. He that despised Moses' law died without mercy under two or three witnesses: Of how much sorer punishment, suppose ye, shall he be thought worthy, who hath trodden under foot the Son of God, and hath counted the blood of the covenant, wherewith he was sanctified, an unholy thing, and hath done despite unto the Spirit of grace? (Heb. 10:26-29)

Here the Bible talks about the choice to receive **peace** with God through **faith** in the efficacy of Jesus' Death and Resurrection or continuance in religious ceremonies and sacrifices in the hope that they will carry us into Rest. In verse 26 of Hebrews 10, he says, "*for if we sin willfully after we have received the knowledge of the truth, there remains no more sacrifice for sins.*" A cursory look at this weighty statement would seem like he was addressing sins like fornication, lying, cheating, stealing, etc. But No, he was not addressing those, even though they are wrong. He was addressing the shift from merely trusting God to take you to the place of rest you once believed he could take you to in Christ, to now using your good deeds in observance of the law as your basis to attain Rest. If this is not clear, do not worry. It will be more apparent by the time you read a bit more.

Understanding the development of the scriptures from Genesis to Malachi, and from the book of Matthew to Revelation is necessary for understanding the purpose of life. As we develop our understanding of the purpose of life, we grow in our certainty of the security that comes through knowledge of God and Jesus Christ. This understanding is a prerequisite to entering the Kingdom of God.

In a previous chapter, we had discussed Noah, Abraham, and Israel. Now we will begin to do a bit more research on the significance of these and other characters to our study.

EPISTEMOLOGY

THE SCRIPTURES ARE BOTH *EXOTERIC* AND *ESOTERIC*. WHEN I refer to scripture as esoteric, I mean that it has a spiritual or moral significance that is not obvious just by reading the scripture. It requires some other faculty beyond the rational mind to comprehend its more profound significance. Usually, the exoteric meaning of scripture is what it means on the surface. The exoteric method of understanding is not what we will primarily concern ourselves with going forward. Many other books and writers have addressed the scriptures at that level. Our intention now is to go deeper. For everything we read about in the *Old Testament* has both an exoteric and esoteric message. The esoteric is more ineffable, so pay careful attention to this part of the book.

The reader must appreciate specific keys. For example, numbers, as used in scripture, have esoteric meanings. Most people are familiar with the famous 666 used in many movies about the end of the world. 666 is the number of Man at his most complete human potential. Can you look at the chart and tell me how we know this? Let us look at some others:

1 – God	2 – Division/Agreement
3 – Completion	4 – Natural Creation
5 – Grace	6 – Man
7 – Perfection	8 – New Beginning
9 – Fruit of Womb and Spirit	10 – Order
11 – Confusion	12 – Divine Government
13 – Rebellion	24 – Complete Priesthood
30 – Maturity	40 – Trial/Tribulation
50 – Jubilee/Freedom	144 – Higher Spiritual Govt.
1000 – Complete Seed	144,000 – Complete Spiritual Govt.

Beyond this, the meaning of numbers usually has significance beyond the comprehension of this author. However, these same numbers raised to the power of their Ten, Hundreds, or Thousands often have a related significance to their single-digit names, but not always. For example, 3 is the Essence of 30. Three means Completion and 30 means Maturity. 2 is not necessarily the essence of 20. 20 is the age at which young Israelites were set apart to God as warriors or numbered citizens. So. in some ways, 20 is a sort of dividing or separating people unto the service of God. In a particular context, it might appear as a derivative of 2, but not always.

4 is the essence of 40. 40 is the number that God uses to signify Trials and Tribulations, while four indicates the natural creation which is at now groaning in pain to be delivered as the Holy Ghost tells us in Romans 8. 5 is the essence of 50. 50 is the number that God uses to signify the year of Freedom or Jubilee, while 5 is the number for Grace. 144 is the number for the stature of Christ. We can see that in Revelations 17:21 because it refers to a man who is an Angel. The only man who can be our "measure" or standard is Jesus Christ. The 144,000 in Revelation 7 and 14 are symbolic of men and women who will grow to become like Christ. The significant thing to understand about the numbers of the spirit is that there is no human formula to use with every number. Context and revelation of the moment must influence what message we think God is speaking through numbers on each occasion. I cannot overemphasize the importance of reliance on prayer concerning this.

If I wrote everything about God's esoteric numbers, I would not finish this book in 120 Years. One Thing that the follower of Christ should beware of concerning numbers is necromancy and Divination. The system of Gematria (the art of ascribing numbers to alphabets to decipher occult meanings) is unbiblical and a subtle gateway to divination. It is not a holy gift from God, but rather an occult method of divination and casting of spells with numbers. In its most benign form, it is merely a scam to make numbers ascribed to alphabets give a pre-determined result to the conjurers. Many well-meaning preachers tell their congregants about how the "Hebrew Alphabets" of the scriptures, when multiplied with other alphabets equate to some special meaning in God. We should avoid this absolute nonsense. It is the beginning of witchcraft.

First, the Hebrew alphabets used in the modern bible schools or among modern Judaic scholars are NOT biblical. These alphabets were created by scholars to replace the long-lost Hebrew language and alphabets referred to as Paleo-Hebrew. Most scholars today believe the Hebrews in Pre-exilic Israel used a variant of the old Phoenician and Egyptian alphabet. Archeological findings of both show strong similarities. *Our* teaching on numbers requires spiritual discernment and not human calculations.

Another factor that has significance in scripture is color. Let us look at some of these:

Green – Life
Blue – Heaven
Purple – Royalty

Red – Suffering
White – Purity

Also, materials have significance. Some examples of these are:

Wood – Humanity
Bronze – Judgment
Gold   Divine Nature
Milk – Exoteric Knowledge
Sea – People
Tail   False Prophet
Star – A Son of God
Moon – The Church
Eye – Knowledge

Iron – Sin
Silver – Redemption
Water – Life
Meat – Esoteric Knowledge
Cloud – Heavenly Host/Persons
Dust – Soul
Sun – The Son of God
Hair – Glory
Bread – Spiritual Word/Thought

Even the animals and birds have significance to be understood by the reader. Biblical scholars often divide animals into Clean and Unclean creatures. Sometimes you will read about the clean creatures being those that "Part the Hoof and Chew the Cud." Any that only does one or none of these is considered unclean.

Sheep – Clean persons that obey the voice of God.
Snakes – Untrustworthy Deceivers

Goats – Clean persons that do whatever they think is best.
Chickens – Persons who should be spiritual but live an earthly and carnal life.

Bats – Spiritual Persons that use Dark Forces of the Occult
Donkeys – Persons who depend solely on empirical knowledge

Lions – Spiritual people with a clean conscience
Vultures – Persons that prey on the unlearned and spiritually dead

Pigs – Persons that pretend to be Sanctimonious, but are unholy.

Eels – Persons who have no scales or fins, and therefore unable to resist the influence of the negativity in the world.

Horse – A spirit

Fish with scales and Fins – Persons who are not influenced by the negativity of the world.

Crabs – Persons who are self-centered and live lowly.

I could say much more about how we know these things, but maybe in another book, we can investigate these things in detail based on scripture, so that your confidence will not rest in our words alone. We have described some of these symbolic meanings with the reader so that you might understand how daunting a task it would be to explain the esoteric meaning of every aspect of the scriptures in our quest to seek an understanding of the Kingdom.

To summarize what we have said so far, let us look at some highlights before we go deeper. We proffer that the purpose of God in creating the universe was to have a home for Man. We went further to state that the reason God creating Man was to have a more suitable home for himself. God placed man in a state of bliss in Eden, but something was missing from man. He had God WITH him, but not IN him. When man sinned against God by disobedience, the home of man became corrupted and rebelled against man himself. Even the very presence of God became unbearable to man, to say nothing of what torment he would have had to endure if God had tried to enter him and dwell in fallen man.

We have said that the fall of man was not a surprise to God, and neither was it unexpected, though it was NOT the intent of God. We realize the complexity of this assertion. The reader will ask, "if God knows all things, and is all-powerful, and knew man would sin; why did he not prevent it?" The answer to this is beyond the comprehension of this writer. Surely, there is an answer. Maybe you could be the person to whom the Lord chooses to reveal this answer. It is not his intention to hide anything forever. He certainly knew man would sin, need a savior, and that you and I would ask ourselves these questions. Therefore, let us speak on those things we have clarity of understanding.

Had man not sinned in the garden of Eden, there would not have been a need for a savior. Neither would there have been an *obvious* need for the indwelling of God in Man by his Holy Spirit. Today we have a hunger for peace and security because of sin and suffering that surrounds us. Had we never sinned in the garden of Eden, would we today require a savior? No, we would not. We would be somewhat akin to angels. However, we need to point out that even though we would not have needed a savior, we would still have required the "Coming of the Lord." The very state we are expecting now. It is this "Coming of the Lord" that we refer to as *entering* the Kingdom.

THE LAW, THE GRACE, AND THE KINGDOM

I WROTE THE PRECEDING CHAPTERS TO GIVE A BASIC UNDERSTANDING of what we understand about what the social and economic environment, based on history, has become for humanity. They were motivated by our desire to help the reader navigate the maze of life and modernity, equipped with the Word of God as an instrument of dissection. Next, we will try to explain the concept of Salvation appropriated through Faith in Jesus Christ, as heralded by the Law, shepherded by the Spirit, and Justified by the judgment to come.

As earlier stated, man is a Soul; he has a spirit and lives in a body. The primary purpose of the creation of humankind is that we might eventually be a suitable habitat for God through His Spirit. Holding this doctrine in mind, let us go on to explain why we cannot deny this assertion.

To complete this, we must put aside, if possible, any biases we have had about God or Salvation. Some of it might have been correct, and most of it might have been wrong. First, the bible scholars among the readership would have noticed that we have defined man as Soul, not a spirit. Why? The bible tells us that God breathed life into man, and so man became a living soul. *"And the LORD God formed man of the dust of the ground, and breathed into his nostrils the breath of life; and man became a living soul"* (Gen. 2:7). Secondly, Jesus is a man. He said to his disciples when he rose from the dead that he was not a spirit.

> *But they were terrified and affrighted, and supposed that they had seen a spirit. And he said unto them, Why are ye troubled? and why do thoughts arise in your hearts? Behold my hands and my feet, that it is I myself: handle me, and see; for a spirit hath not flesh and bones, as ye see me have. And when he had thus spoken, he shewed them his hands and his feet. And while they yet believed not for joy, and wondered, he said unto them, Have ye here*

any meat? And they gave him a piece of a broiled fish, and of an honeycomb. And he took it, and did eat before them. (Luke 24:37-43).

Also, when he died on the cross, he said, *"Father, into your hands I commit my spirit."* He did not say "soul" because his soul went somewhere else:

And it was about the sixth hour, and there was a darkness over all the earth until the ninth hour. And the sun was darkened, and the veil of the temple was rent in the midst. And when Jesus had cried with a loud voice, he said, Father, into thy hands I commend my spirit: and having said thus, he gave up the ghost (Luke 23:46-47).

In our discussion on the fallacy of evolution, the reader will remember that we stated that while it is possible for animals to "evolve" *within* its Genus, man can only evolve spiritually. Physically, he can adapt but not evolve. This fallacy is essential to understand because the intention of God was for man to evolve from a natural soul to a spiritual soul. In Genesis chapter One, the twenty-sixth verse states that *"let us make man in our image, after our LIKENESS."* However, in the very next verse, it says, *"so God created man in his IMAGE, in the IMAGE of God created he him; male and female created he them."* Notice that his purpose was to make them not ONLY to be in his image, as all men are but also to be LIKE him, as few men will be:

Behold, what manner of love the Father hath bestowed upon us, that we should be called the sons of God: therefore the world knoweth us not, because it knew him not. Beloved, now are we the sons of God, and it doth not yet appear what we shall be: but we know that, when he shall appear, we shall be like him; for we shall see him as he is (1st Jn. 3:1-2).

The first chapter of Genesis is where we find the declaration of the intent of God, and the actions that inspired this statement. "things that were not as though they were":

Therefore it is of faith, that it might be by grace; to the end the promise might be sure to all the seed; not to that only which is of the law, but to that also which is of the faith of Abraham; who is the father of us all, (As it is written, I have made thee a father of many nations,) before him whom he believed, even God, who quickeneth the dead, <u>and calleth those things which be not as though they were</u> (Rom. 4:17).

In the second chapter of Genesis, we see the actual procedure by which the forming of Man BEGAN. Chapter Five indicates to us that within the created man, there was a woman (Eve) waiting to be brought forth at the appropriate time:

> *This is the book of the generations of Adam. In the day that God created man, in the likeness of God made he him; Male and female created he them; and blessed them, and called their name Adam, in the day when they were created* (Gen. 5:1-2).

He called BOTH their name ADAM. It was the man that named his wife Eve, not God.

Next, we see the man given a Law by God not to eat of a tree. It is my submission that had God NOT given that Law, man would have lived forever without getting old or sick. It was the *consciousness* of the Law itself that provoked the possibility and subsequent engagement in the act of rebellion. However, since without this act, there would have been no Sin; without the Sin, there would have been no sickness or death. If there were no sickness or death, there would have been no need for a savior. Without a savior, there would have been no hope of a Resurrection. Without the resurrection, there would have been no conformity into his LIKENESS. He had died and rose from death before the world began. *"And all that dwell upon the earth shall worship him, whose names are not written in the book of life of the Lamb slain from the foundation of the world"* (Rev. 13:8). Also, the Acts of the Apostles contains a similar statement. *"Known unto God are all his works from the beginning of the world"* (Acts 15:18).

If we hold in mind that God had one Son, but that he intended to bring forth many sons, we will understand that one needed to die so that many could come into Sonship (The Kingdom). Jesus himself articulated this profoundly when he said, *"Verily, verily, I say unto you, except a corn of wheat fall into the ground and die, it abideth alone: but if it dies, it bringeth forth much fruit."* (Jn 12:24). Therefore, death is a necessary pathway to the life of God. The death of Jesus was the pathway through which God would change the body of Jesus from an ordinary flesh and blood body to a glorious Christ-like body. As the Apostle Paul puts it, *"Who shall change our vile body, that it may be fashioned like unto his glorious body, according to the working whereby he is able even to subdue all things unto himself."* (Philippians 3:21).

So, we see that nothing happens by accident with God. The mistake that Eve made, coupled with Adam's disobedience (she was deceived, he was disobedient) granted legitimacy to the intervention of the Son of God in the person of the beautiful Master, Jesus Christ. It was all a plan by God to create an avenue by which he could make man into, not just his image, but also his Likeness. This process is currently ongoing; he has not finished making Man.

Ultimately then, the purpose of creating man was in preparation for the "Coming of the Lord." The intent is to bring to this Universe, the qualities and nature of the "Kingdom of Heaven." This Kingdom of Heaven is a realm in which everything works and moves in complete harmony with the Will of God. While Heaven is the home of God, the natural universe is the home of man. For God to dwell in it, he would have to become a man, or at least take on the nature of man. Heaven is not the permanent domicile of man. This universe is supposed to be the eternal home of man. *"And God said, Let us make man in our image, after our likeness: and let them have dominion over the fish of the sea, and over the fowl of the air, and over the cattle, and over all the earth, and over every creeping thing that creepeth upon the earth "*(Gen. 1:26). Even at the end of the bible, we see God himself coming to earth to dwell WITH man, rather than man going to Heaven to dwell with God. *"And I saw a new heaven and a new earth: for the first heaven and the first earth were passed away; and there was no more sea. And I John saw the holy city, new Jerusalem, coming down from God out of heaven, prepared as a bride adorned for her husband. And I heard a great voice out of heaven saying, Behold, the tabernacle of God is with men, and he will dwell with them, and they shall be his people, and God himself shall be with them, and be their God"* (Rev. 21:1-3).

It is imperative to understand that often when the scriptures speak about the Earth, it is referring to Man. "And the LORD God formed man of the dust of the ground, and breathed into his nostrils the breath of life; and man became a living soul" (Gen. 2:7.) In the book of Ecclesiastes, there is a similar scripture hinting at this truth also. "All go unto one place; all are of the dust, and all turn to dust again"(Eccl. 3:20). And yet again, in the Proverbs, we read Wisdom describing Man as the highest Dust of the Earth:

> *I was set up from everlasting, from the beginning, or ever the earth was. When there were no depths, I was brought forth; when there were no fountains abounding with water. Before the mountains were settled, before the hills was I brought forth While as yet he had not made the earth, nor the fields, nor the highest part of the dust of the world* (Prov. 8:26).

This passage is another example of an allegorical symbol that indicates some spiritual meaning though referencing something natural. So, the context of these scriptures, refer to man and not to the natural dust under your feet.

Man is transforming into a permanent, and "Acceptable" habitation for God:

Now therefore ye are no more strangers and foreigners, but fellow citizens with the saints, and of the household of God; And are built upon the foundation of the apostles and prophets, Jesus Christ himself being the chief corner stone; In whom all the building fitly framed together groweth unto an holy temple in the Lord: In whom ye also are builded together for an habitation of God through the Spirit (Eph. 2:19-22).

If there is one crucial thing you need to understand about every story and account in the bible, it is that they all symbolically are referring to this plan of God; his intent to make you and I a habitation suitable for him.

After the bible's creation account and the general genealogy of the peoples of the earth, the sixth chapter of the Book of Genesis has an account of something that seems to be of concern to God. It is the intermarriage between "*The sons of God and the daughters of men*":

And it came to pass, when men began to multiply on the face of the earth, and daughters were born unto them, That the sons of God saw the daughters of men that they were fair; and they took them wives of all which they chose. And the LORD said, My spirit shall not always strive with man, for that he also is flesh: yet his days shall be an hundred and twenty years. There were giants in the earth in those days; and also after that, when the sons of God came in unto the daughters of men, and they bare children to them, the same became mighty men which were of old, men of renown (Gen. 6:1-4).

These "sons of God" were NOT Angels, as many unlearned persons often teach. These were men who had a Godly ancestry and possessed a God-consciousness. They were intermarrying with women who did not have the same appreciation and knowledge of God, both in themselves and from the ancestral background that they came from:

And Adam knew his wife again; and she bare a son, and called his name Seth: For God, said she, hath appointed me another seed instead of Abel, whom Cain slew. And to Seth, to him also there was born a son; and he called his name Enos: then began men to call upon the name of the LORD (Gen. 4:25-26).

From these scriptures, we can see that until a son was born to Seth, people had not begun calling unto God. Also, Jesus clearly says that Angels neither marry nor are they given in marriage. "Jesus *answered and said unto them, Ye do err, not knowing the scriptures, nor the power of God. For in the resurrection they neither marry, nor are given in marriage, but are as the angels of God in heaven*" (Matt. 22:29-30).

Now, what is the spiritual significance of this story? It principally is indicating that a person without a belief in Christ does not have the possibility of becoming one with him or his people. There is a barrier that never allows the relationship to harmonize into what God ordained for a man and woman, the two becoming ONE with him.

In courtship, it is more important to know that the person you want to marry doesn't only profess to believe in Christ if you are one who believes, but you should be sure you understand HOW the person believes. You must know the degree of commitment the person has to spiritual matters in Christ relative to yours. Just the fact that a person professes with their mouth is no evidence that they have believed in their heart. Sadly, they can pretend for years and almost ruin your calling. Fortunately, God has so much invested in your ministry that he will find a way to bail you out at the last moment. Believe Me!

However, there are other "unions" that you can enter with people that have nothing to do with marriage, but to which this scripture in the sixth chapter of Genesis still applies. For example, if you want to go into business or contract with a person that does not believe, you must make sure that your agreement allows you to get out unconditionally or puts you in a dominant decision-making position. Therefore the very same chapter that tells a believer not to go to secular Courts with another believer says this:

> Be ye not unequally yoked together with unbelievers: for what fellowship hath righteousness with unrighteousness? and what communion hath light with darkness? And what concord hath Christ with Belial? or what part hath he that believeth with an infidel? (2 Cor. 6:14-15).

That is why the Apostle Paul says you should not be "unequally yoked with a non-believer." They might have a better moral character than you, but their soul and spirit are not subject to the spirit of God as yours might be.

These unions can also exist between you and organizations. For example, Credit Card contracts, Home Loans, Car loans, etc. are examples of being unequally yoked. So, you can see the exoteric and esoteric nature of the Word of Christ at play again. Living a life SEPERATED as much as possible from worldly entanglements is fulfilling the requirement of not "marrying" the daughters of men.

There was a judgment on the earth in those times because of the sons of God marrying those women. God poured a great flood upon all the earth. In this flood, God saved only eight people: Noah and his family. Go back to our list of the spiritual meaning of numbers and see again what the number 8 symbolizes! Now that we can see that there was a natural flood that brought upon destruction as punishment for being yoked with unbelievers, what do you think would be the consequence to us for entangling ourselves with all the things we just mentioned? The judgment has already begun. Do you see the condition of the world today? Can you see how indebtedness has ruined not only individuals but even nations? People are trapped, and so are those who were supposed to know better and put our trust in Christ. We are experiencing the judgment, just as Noah himself did. He lost all his property and friends and cousins, etc. Noah was such a lonely and sad man that he drank himself into a stupor, even though God had saved him. *"And Noah began to be an husbandman, and he planted a vineyard: And he drank of the wine, and was drunken; and he was uncovered within his tent"* (Gen. 9:20-21). Look around you; each day, someone you know is being taken away by the "flood."

As time went on, the descendants of Noah repopulated the earth. As they began to become more abundant in number, they showed concern for maintaining some form of unity through building a City and a Tower whose top might go into the Height of the skies. The scriptures do not give us an exact measurement of how high they wanted to go, but we know one thing; they did NOT even begin to build it. God took away the universal language they had, and they could no longer understand each other. So, they left off building the City:

> *And the whole earth was of one language, and of one speech. And it came to pass, as they journeyed from the east, that they found a plain in the land of Shinar; and they dwelt there. And they said one to another, Go to, let us make brick, and burn them thoroughly. And they had brick for stone, and slime had they for morter. And they said, Go to, let us build us a city and a tower, whose top may reach unto heaven; and let us make us a name, lest we be scattered abroad upon the face of the whole earth. And the LORD came down to see the city and the tower, which the children of men builded. And the LORD said, Behold, the people is one, and they have all one language; and this they begin to do: and now nothing will be restrained from them, which they have imagined to do. Go to, let us go down, and there confound their language, that they may not understand one another's speech. So the LORD scattered them abroad from thence upon the face of all the earth: and they left off to build the city. Therefore, is the name of it called Babel; because the LORD did there confound the language of all the earth: and from thence did the LORD scatter them abroad upon the face of all the earth* (Gen. 11:1-9).

The esoteric meaning of this story is about the rebellious soul of man. God had said in the very beginning that Man should be fruitful and multiply on the face of the earth, but these guys thought they had a better idea. It is the same today. Christ left us with a free will and a commandment to love all men. However, we have established denominations in his name, claiming they are from him. We categorize anyone who is not a member of our sect as not being our "brother." We have established countries and delineated the borders by our will. Anyone not from within those borders is considered an "other." All these acts of ours conform with the allegory of the "Tower of Babel."

The law intended to help us navigate the pitfalls of our destruction, but ended up becoming a snare against us. This fact is alluded to so many times in the gospels by Jesus in his disputing of the Pharisees. The law is a curse when not understood as an informational manual rather than an end itself. Even now, in the era of Christ's Grace, many who believe in Christ live under the law's curse in attempting to please God by willfully observing the Law. They make it a duty to set aside ten percent of their income in hopes of "staving off the devourer." They set aside special days for the commemoration of biblical events, even though neither the Spirit of God nor Jesus Christ made any such requirement. As benign as these things are for a young believer, the consequences for those who should know better is the stunting of their spiritual growth.

A NEW NATION

GOD IS RAISING A NEW NATION COMPRISED OF PEOPLE FROM multiple denominations or religions. They recognize the necessity of a Savior in their lives and the potency of the sacrifice of Christ. They are coming out from Islam, Judaism, Christianity, Buddhism, Communism, Capitalism, Socialism, etc. etc. to the Living God, in the person of Jesus Christ. We should not, as I once did, equate "Christianity" with Faith in Jesus Christ. "Christianity" is a set of rituals and principles begun at the end of the 1st century CE by people often referred to as "Neo-Platonists."

The cultural expressions of the Mediterranean peoples of the early 1st century are the foundation for most of the "Christian" belief systems. In some ways, it is a cultural imposition that obfuscates the simplicity of the Gospel of Christ. God wants people to lose all fear and come to him as any father beckons a child. He does not need an intermediary between himself and you. He has made himself the intermediary in the person of Christ:

> *I exhort therefore, that, first of all, supplications, prayers, intercessions, and giving of thanks, be made for all men; For kings, and for all that are in authority; that we may lead a quiet and peaceable life in all godliness and honesty. For this is good and acceptable in the sight of God our Saviour; Who will have all men to be saved, and to come unto the knowledge of the truth. For there is one God, and one mediator between God and men, the man Christ Jesus; Who gave himself a ransom for all, to be testified in due time* (1st Tim. 2:1-6).

When we read the above-referenced passage, we can see that the "Christ Jesus" referred to there is a "group of people" who have the authority to intercede on behalf of temporal powers. What this means is that everyone who has the anointing of Christ in their hearts and minds can bring change to the earthly realm. The mindset of those misled in their understanding of "Christ" hinders the manifestation of this reality. *"For as in Adam all die, even so in Christ shall all be made alive. But every man in his own order: Christ the firstfruits; afterward they that are Christ's at his coming* (1 Cor. 15:22-23). Notice that "Christ" is pluralized.

The citizens of the Kingdom of God are a nation within nations. What distinguishes them from other Christians is that they are elected to partake in "the First Resurrection." First as in Quality, and not first as in Chronology:

> *And I saw thrones, and they sat upon them, and judgment was given unto them: and I saw the souls of them that were beheaded for the witness of Jesus, and for the word of God, and which had not worshipped the beast, neither his image, neither had received his mark upon their foreheads, or in their hands; and they lived and reigned with Christ a thousand years. But the rest of the dead lived not again until the thousand years were finished. This is the first resurrection. Blessed and holy is he that hath part in the first resurrection: on such the second death hath no power, but they shall be priests of God and of Christ and shall reign with him a thousand years* (Rev. 20:4-6).

The Resurrection is not just an event. The resurrection is a personality. It is the manifestation of the character of Christ. As you take on this personality, you become "Christlike". After this morphology, you "Win" the status of Christ:

> *Then said Martha unto Jesus, Lord, if thou hadst been here, my brother had not died. But I know, that even now, whatsoever thou wilt ask of God, God will give it thee. Jesus saith unto her, Thy brother shall rise again. Martha saith unto him, I know that he shall rise again in the resurrection at the last day. Jesus said unto her, I am the resurrection, and the life: he that believeth in me, though he were dead, yet shall he live: And whosoever liveth and believeth in me shall never die. Believest thou this?* (Jn. 11:21-26).

From this statement of Jesus to Martha, we can see clearly from his mouth that "the resurrection" is a person.

In another scripture, God shows us that Christ is a status that people can win. It is the goal of faith. Heaven has already been attained as I have already demonstrated in previous chapters:

> *But what things were gain to me, those I counted loss for Christ. Yea doubtless, and I count all things but loss for the excellency of the knowledge of Christ Jesus my Lord: for whom I have suffered the loss of all things, and do count them but dung, that I may win Christ, And be found in him, not having mine own righteousness, which is of the law, but that*

which is through the faith of Christ, the righteousness which is of God by faith: That I may know him, and the power of his resurrection, and the fellowship of his sufferings, being made conformable unto his death; If by any means I might attain unto the resurrection of the dead (Phil. 3:7-11).

We can see that even Paul is speaking here about his desire to ATTAIN to a Resurrection. This resurrection cannot be the general resurrection, because that is going to be made available to all that believe through faith in Christ. However, he is here speaking about a different, EARNED, resurrection. All who attain to this earned resurrection, achieve Christ.

I could say more about this, but this part of the book is an introduction to a deeper understanding of Christ. Perhaps in future editions, I will be able to elaborate more on this aspect of the Kingdom. To be found worthy of this Christ status, we must be willing to sacrifice earthly Rights and privileges. We must be willing to accept our family and loved ones turn their back on us. We must be willing to leave our motherland and fatherland to go to a place about which we know nothing. It is a journey we must sometimes travel alone, but at no time shall we be lonely. It is the journey to Christ. The voyage into the Kingdom of God.

What God did with a man named Abram demonstrates this figuratively. The scriptures say that God called him out of his father's house, and from his fatherland to a place he would show him. He tested him and gave him and his wife new names. Names in scripture have an esoteric meaning. They refer to a character trait that God or whoever does the naming sees or expects to see in an individual or circumstance. You are like Abraham. Today God is calling you out from all you have known, into something deeper and more meaningful. That voice in you that has told you there is something higher is waiting on you. There are other voices of doubt, fear, and mockery. The truth is, "what do you have to lose"? Listen to the voice of God through his Son. Ask him to speak and guide you, and he will. Not only will he do that. He will make you see that he just saved you from the "flood."

FROM ABRAHAM TO JESUS

IRST THROUGH ADAM, AND LATER NOAH, GOD SOUGHT TO RAISE A people amongst whom he would dwell and commune. None were worthy until God found Abraham. He was to be the vessel through whom God would establish a nation. This nation was "set apart," unique and powerful. Through Abraham, a "Seed," meaning Christ, would be born, and through Christ, a whole generation of spiritual Sons would become a final habitation for God. *"Ye also, as lively stones, are built up a spiritual house, a holy priesthood, to offer up spiritual sacrifices, acceptable to God by Jesus Christ."* (1 Pet. 2:5) This re-birth is the basis of the phrase "Born Again."

Earlier in this book, we briefly mentioned Africa is central to understanding an anthropomorphic God and its relevance in interpreting much of the significant conceptualizations and idiosyncrasies of biblical characters. While the idea of gods was prevalent in all societies, the concept of a single Omniscient and Omnipresent God, served by other lesser gods, is primarily an African concept. Whether it be in Greek or Roman culture, we can only find a reference to anthropomorphic gods who had passions similar to men. It appears that the idea of an omnipresent God was not a part of the spiritual development of those regions during antiquity. Even Pharaoh Akhenaten drew the wrath of the Egyptian priests when he commanded people to only worship the One God. The priests of Egypt knew there was the omniscient and omnipresent God. What they disagreed about with Pharoah Akhnaten about was that the people should only worship this One God neglecting the other lesser gods. At this stage, it is essential to point out a significant difference between religion as practiced in the African/Abrahamic context, as compared to what was practiced in other parts of the world then, especially in Europe and Asia.

Abraham and the patriarchs were "African" in their cosmogonic outlook on the supernatural. By this, I mean that God was to them a tribal God. In the sense that you worshipped him in different ways depending on to what tribe you belonged. You could not be his worshipper if you were not from their tribe by birth. People expected you to worship him according to your customs and traditions as inherited from the tribe of your forefathers. You could not be his worshipper if you were not from their tribe by birth. They were not into proselytizing people into their religion. That is the primary distinction between African spirituality and the rest. In rare instances, you might offer devotions and offerings to their god or some other god on an as-needed basis, but each nation or tribe had their god, and no one else could claim him, which is a practice we find only in Africa. Each tribe has its god, and you cannot come from another tribe and assume that the god of the foreign tribe has any obligation to you. *"For this God is our God for ever and ever: he will be our guide even unto death "*(Ps. 48:14).

So, when God came to Abraham, he introduced himself with a name for identification. That name was *El Shaddai*. God did this to help Abraham and to clarify that he was not to be confused with any other deity. So, unlike today when people go around trying to convert people to their religion and God, this practice would have seemed foolish to the biblical patriarchs. Abraham, Moses, Jonah, and others would have been surprised to see all the people of the world, claiming "their" God as that of everyone else. God Jehovah was *their* God, and theirs alone. We see much later the Prophet Jonah get angry with God for saving the Assyrian city of Nineveh because he felt Jehovah was only supposed to save Israel. Of course, God is the God of every nation on earth.

This understanding is necessary to be able to appropriately decipher the mindset of Abraham as he begins his relationship with God. He needed a child, but his wife had been unable to conceive. He had wealth and riches but no heir to continue his lineage after he was gone. So, God made him a **promise** of a special child. According to the Apostle Paul, that child was Christ. Isaac, Abraham's physical child, was simply a typological figure of Abraham's true "Seed," Christ Jesus. *"Now to Abraham and his seed were the promises made. He saith not, And to seeds, as of many; but as of one, And to thy seed, which is Christ"* (Gal. 3:16).

Even though Abraham believed God, as time went on, he and his wife began to lose hope as they saw themselves getting older and having no child. His wife, Sarah, suggested he copulate with her maid since she, Sarah, was too old to conceive naturally. A child was born from the union and is named Ishmael. However, this was not the child that God promised. God insisted that the child must come through Sarah. Abraham begged God not to continue testing his faith but just to accept Ishmael. God insisted that Isaac would be born later by Sarah. Abraham continued to believe God, and at the appointed time, Sarah conceived and had Isaac. When the two children began to grow, Sarah became concerned about the place of her son and insisted that Abraham send away his son Ishmael and the mother. He was sad to do so, but God told him to listen to his wife, promising to take care of Ishmael for Abraham.

At one point, God tested Abraham to see if he would give up everything for God. He asked Abraham to take Isaac to a mountain and kill him as a sacrifice to God. As Abraham was about to do so, God stopped him and said he would make Abraham great for his obedience to God. Isaac grew up to become the father of Esau and Jacob. His son Jacob became the father of twelve sons, who became the ancestors of the twelve tribes of Israel. God had changed Jacob's name to Israel. Once again, the experiences of these bible characters have both exoteric and esoteric meanings. It is essential to see the Word of God as a multi-dimensional emanation of the Will of God. Its first emanation is Natural; therefore, it means what it says and says what it means. The second dimension has Moral meaning. The third level has a Spiritual significance. Once you have the Keys to appreciating the Word of God, you will often be able to decipher the hidden message in some of the stories and accounts of the characters and events written.

In the story of Abraham, the three patriarchs, Abraham, Isaac, and Jacob, are symbolic of the Triune God, Father, Son, and Holy Spirit. We can observe the father (Abraham) offering up his son (Isaac) to die on the Holy Mountain, just as God offered up the Lord Jesus to die for us on the mount named Golgotha. We see the twelve tribes come out of the loins of Jacob just as the Holy Spirit came down from Jesus:

> *This Jesus hath God raised up, whereof we all are witnesses. Therefore being by the right hand of God exalted, and having received of the Father the promise of the Holy Ghost, he hath <u>shed forth this</u>, which ye now see and hear* (Acts.2:32-33).

Even when Abraham and Isaac climbed the mountain for the sacrifice, Abraham laid the bunch of wood on the back of Isaac, which was a foreshadowing of how Jesus would carry the Cross up the mountain. *Wood is symbolic of Humanity.* When Abraham passed the test by demonstrating his willingness to obey God and sacrifice his only Son, he was shown a Ram caught by its horns in the <u>thicket</u> of a bush, which is another spiritual symbol of the Crown of <u>thorns</u> placed on the head of Jesus.

Isaac, who allegorically represents Christ Jesus, is said to have had two sons, Esau and Jacob. Esau was the firstborn, and according to tradition, he was supposed to be the inheritor of the promise of God to Abraham. However, he not having much regard nor appreciation of the value of it, traded it to his younger brother for a meal:

> And Jacob sod pottage: and Esau came from the field, and he was faint: And Esau said to Jacob, Feed me, I pray thee, with that same red pottage; for I am faint: therefore was his name called Edom. And Jacob said, Sell me this day thy birthright. And Esau said, Behold, I am at the point to die: and what profit shall this birthright do to me? And Jacob said, Swear to me this day; and he sware unto him: and he sold his birthright unto Jacob. Then Jacob gave Esau bread and pottage of lentiles; and he did eat and drink, and rose up, and went his way: thus Esau despised his birthright (Gen. 25:29-34).

Years later, when his father was about to die, he went to obtain the blessing of the First Son, but his father told him that the younger had taken it. He cried and demanded his father find some blessing for him also. He got one, but not the blessing of the First Born.

Now this story has a moral and a spiritual significance. Let us deal with the spiritual significance of it. This story communicates to the initiate that there is a divine purpose for those who come later to Christ, even though those who came first should have received the Promise. In the first instance, those who came first are natural Israel in the bible, and those who came later are the Christians of the New Testament. However, even today, the struggle exists between the believer in Christ with an old mindset versus their emerging new mindset. The old being the legalistic mind, and the new being the graceful mind. So the Christians who think that because of their good deeds they are more acceptable to God, risk missing the end time reward that Jesus will give to those who continued to grow in him through Faith, and not through good deeds.

For this reason, the Apostle Paul talks about a physical transformation taking place in the individual based on the renewing of her mind:

> I beseech you therefore, brethren, by the mercies of God, that ye present your bodies a living sacrifice, holy, acceptable unto God, which is your reasonable service. And be not conformed to this world: but be ye transformed by the renewing of your mind, that ye may prove what is that good, and acceptable, and perfect, will of God (Rom. 12:1-2)

Also, in the second book of Corinthians, we see how those who allow the transformation of themselves by faith, receive a glory inaccessible to others. *"But we all, with open face beholding as in a glass the glory of the Lord, are changed into the same image from glory to glory, even as by the Spirit of the Lord. "*(2 Cor. 3:18).

Jacob gave Birth to twelve sons. If we remember what the number 12 represents in our table, then we can understand why Israel (the twelve tribes) were at that time, the chosen people. Twelve is the number for the divine government. They were to be a light to the world in the knowledge of God:

> *Thou hast avouched the LORD this day to be thy God, and to walk in his ways, and to keep his statutes, and his commandments, and his judgments, and to hearken unto his voice: And the LORD hath avouched thee this day to be his peculiar people, as he hath promised thee, and that thou shouldest keep all his commandments; And to make thee high above all nations which he hath made, in praise, and in name, and in honour; and that thou mayest be an holy people unto the LORD thy God, as he hath spoken* (Deut. 26:17-19).

When Jesus came, he did not just arbitrarily choose the number 12 for his Apostles. As mentioned earlier, it is the number for Divine Government. Sometimes in scripture, you will notice the number 144 or 144,000. These are also analogous to Divine Government as they are multiple of 12. *"And I heard the number of them which were sealed: and there were sealed an hundred and forty and four thousand of all the tribes of the children of Israel"* (Rev. 7:4). Israel mentioned here in Revelation is not the other Israel of the old testament that descended from Jacob.

As you can see, in the list that follows verse 4, the tribe of Dan is excised while Joseph is included with his son Manasseh. The reason why is beyond the scope of this book.

Scripture contains the names of all twelve brothers, but for this section, we would like to discuss one. This person is the 11th child, Joseph. If you recall what we said about the number 11, then you will realize that his kidnapping and sale into slavery, introduced confusion into the house of Jacob. However, after many years in Egypt, he rose from being a slave to becoming Prime Minister of Egypt, and second only to Pharaoh. The moral of the story is that no matter what a destined life is going through, God has an intent to bless him and his community through the temporary suffering.

Spiritually the story of Joseph speaks to something more profound, and its significance might not be easy to understand. All twelve brothers represent the believers in Christ, but Joseph represents a sub-set of the believers chosen to enter the Kingdom, which is the deeper meaning of almost all the scripture. The idea is that there is a higher position available to some foreordained persons and that this position is not open to every believer.

For whom he did foreknow, he also did predestinate to be conformed to the image of his Son, that he might be the firstborn among many brethren. Moreover whom he did predestinate, them he also-called: and whom he called, them he also justified: and whom he justified, them he also glorified. What shall we then say to these things? If God be for us, who can be against us? He that spared not his own Son, but delivered him up for us all, how shall he not with him also freely give us all things? Who shall lay any thing to the charge of God's elect? It is God that justifieth (Rom. 8:29-33).

So today, there are believers in Christ who will not enter the kingdom because they were not "Predestined" to. (Even among those predestined to, many will fail to make it), which is articulated clearly in Romans, chapter 8. Most people have, unfortunately, thought that it was referring to our salvation. Salvation is a gift, but entering the Kingdom is an opportunity given to a few.

And the disciples came, and said unto him, Why speakest thou unto them in parables? He answered and said unto them, Because it is given unto you to know the mysteries of the kingdom of heaven, but to them it is not given. For whosoever hath, to him shall be given, and he shall have more abundance: but whosoever hath not, from him shall be taken away even that he hath (Matt. 13:10-12).

After Joseph and his 11 brothers are dead and buried, their descendants who had come into Egypt to settle during the rule of Joseph became a targeted group by the new Pharaoh. The descendants of Jacob and his twelve sons had only been in Egypt for roughly over a hundred years before this change in policy occurred, not four hundred years, as many bible scholars believe. According to the Apostle Paul, it was four hundred and thirty years from the time God gave a promise to Abraham and the time that he gave the Laws to Moses. The King James Version of the Old Testament mistakenly refers to the period as four hundred years.

Now to Abraham and his seed were the promises made. He saith not, And to seeds, as of many; but as of one, And to thy seed, which is Christ. And this I say, that the covenant, that was confirmed before of God in Christ, the law, which was four hundred and thirty years after, cannot disannul, that it should make the promise of none effect. For if the inheritance be of the law, it is no more of promise: but God gave it to Abraham by promise (Gal. 3:16-18).

The spiritual significance of this story regarding the persecution of Israel by Pharaoh is related to the unique persons who exist today but do not conform to the mindset of the current world system. These are they that will be considered worthy to enter the Kingdom. These persons are believers who have seen the degeneracy accepted and glorified by the governments and systems of the world and have chosen to separate themselves from it and to speak out against it. <u>These people can expect to be targeted for assassinations covertly and overtly</u> because we live in the time and hour of the Anti-Christ, but most people cannot see it. They are expecting one man to come and physically declare himself to be Anti-Christ. They do not understand that it is a spiritual phenomenon that shall and has taken over the world:

> *And he causeth all, both small and great, rich and poor, free and bond, to receive a mark in their right hand, or in their foreheads: And that no man might buy or sell, save he that had the mark, or the name of the beast, or the number of his name* (Rev. 13:16-17)

The suffering and hardships people experience in the world causes them to conform to the debauchery because they need to feed themselves and their families. However, people shall arise, just as Moses did, to challenge this wickedness.

THE JOURNEY FROM RELIGION

A FTER JUST OVER A HUNDRED YEARS IN EGYPT, THE ISRAELITES found themselves maltreated by a King who was NOT of Egyptian, but Assyrian Ancestry:

For thus saith the LORD, Ye have sold yourselves for nought; and ye shall be redeemed without money. For thus saith the Lord GOD, My people went down aforetime into Egypt to sojourn there; and the Assyrian oppressed them without cause (Is. 52:3-4).

It was during the reign of this foreign King that Egyptians maltreated the Hebrews (meaning Israelites and other settlers). These foreigners we now know to be referred to as the "Shepherd Kings" or "Hyksos." From ancient records, we know that they ruled southern Egypt (The Nile Flows upwards) for about 100-120 years, and then they were driven from Egypt by the Cushite from modern Sudan who came and established the 18th Dynasty.

About the end of this Hyksos rule of Egypt, Moses was born. He was raised and schooled in all the Priestly Knowledge of the Egyptians.

But when the time of the promise drew nigh, which God had sworn to Abraham, the people grew and multiplied in Egypt, Till another king arose, which knew not Joseph. The same dealt subtilly with our kindred, and evil entreated our fathers, so that they cast out their young children, to the end they might not live. In which time Moses was born, and was exceeding fair, and nourished up in his father's house three months: And when he was cast out, Pharaoh's daughter took him up, and nourished him for her own son. And Moses was learned in all the wisdom of the Egyptians, and was mighty in words and in deeds (Acts 7:17-22).

Religion was the foundation of Egyptian education. It was a forty-year training, so the fact the bible states that Moses was Forty years old when he "came of age" is significant. Ordinarily, men came of age much earlier than that in ancient Egypt if we are referring to just chronological age. What is meant in this particular situation is that Moses had attained knowledge into the mystery schools of Egypt. These details are important to understand because this man Moses would serve as an Archetype of a "savior people" to come in our time. Some Bible teachers refer to these people as the "First Fruits Company."

The life of Moses is exemplary of a people who have opportunity to be "successful" in this life's understanding but choose to give up the allure of wealth and splendor if need be for the sake of a higher calling:

> By faith Moses, when he was come to years, refused to be called the son of Pharaoh's daughter; Choosing rather to suffer affliction with the people of God, than to enjoy the pleasures of sin for a season; Esteeming the reproach of Christ greater riches than the treasures in Egypt: for he had respect unto the recompense of the reward (Heb.11:24-26).

Now, let us analyze the spiritual significance of this story as it relates to you and me. As we said earlier, Moses is an archetype of the people who shall be born and manifested during this time in which we live. They will see the bondage of Sin that men and women are in, and they shall come with a Word and Power that will bring transformation to the earth. These people are symbolically described as the "Two Witnesses" in the Apocalypse. They are not just two individuals, as portrayed in some deceptive "Christian" movies, but are representative of a peculiar group of people.

So as not to be misunderstood, it is important to state that the very first enemy that we must overcome is within our being. We must first overcome, by the power of Christ, the inhibitions that keep us bound to iniquities. The struggle is to overcome the flesh and institute the Kingdom of God in our bodies. This struggle is not conducted through Will power but by patient dependence on the subtle, unobservable, and transformative power of Christ through his Spirit. However, in trying to accomplish this, we will discover that there will be unavoidable conflict without also. The outside world has laid its foundation in uncleanliness and greed. Any attempt to try to turn people away from that lifestyle is a direct attack on the financial security of many powerful figures in society. There are both spiritual and temporal forces to lock horns with: *"For we wrestle not against flesh and blood, but against principalities, against powers, against the rulers of the darkness of this world, against spiritual wickedness in high places"* (Eph. 6:12).

The religious institutions, as well as the political and financial institutions, are agencies by which wicked men and spiritual forces impose unnatural conduct upon mankind to make mankind uninhabitable for God. They are uninhabitable due to the spiritual stench that God must endure from the uncleansed, which is the actual struggle. However, very few of the men in religious, political, or financial influence worldwide know the real purpose for which they have received the powers that they wield on earth. As we go along, we will address more about how people use religion to perpetuate sin and unrighteousness in the world, and less about the political and financial dimension of this unrighteousness.

One of the things Christ came to save us from is Religion. Most people would be horrified to hear that, but all you need do is read the account of the life of Jesus, and you will see that his constant opponents were the religiously minded people of his day. It was they who took him to Pontius Pilate, and it is they who today will betray the Elect Sons of God. Those of us who know the path to the Kingdom will do well to be wary of these "religious" people. They remain under the wrath of God because they deny the simplicity of the Gospel. They would rather keep in chains, poor and innocent people searching for God. They do this because of the financial reward. Many others do it for reasons that we wish we did not have to mention, Child sex abuse, human sacrifice, false miracles for money, etc.

Do you think the scandals of sex abuse in the Catholic church are just isolated events by some rogue Priests? Don't you know it is abnormal for a man to say he will live his whole life without a woman? The bible refers to such abstinence as a "doctrine of devils:"

> *Now the Spirit speaketh expressly, that in the latter times some shall depart from the faith, giving heed to seducing spirits, and doctrines of devils; Speaking lies in hypocrisy; having their conscience seared with a hot iron; Forbidding to marry, and commanding to abstain from meats, which God hath created to be received with thanksgiving of them which believe and know the truth* (1 Tim. 4:1-3).

Such a forced practice is dangerous because it sanctions iniquities hidden in the guise of celibacy, to the destruction of souls of children through child sexual abuse. The wrath of God came upon those who participated in such wickedness in the scriptures. You must ask God to give you direction and courage on how to escape the wrath. It certainly is not an easy decision to make when you must leave such organizations calling themselves "churches." However, remember the cries and tears of the little children who innocently went to the monasteries to pray, but ended up being raped consistently by adult men.

For those who claim to practice the Islamic religion, you also must ask yourself a big question. Certainly, the world wronged many people, but how can it be reasonable that only the poor among you lose their limbs for the same crime that the rich get a slap on the wrists? Do you think God does not see? When you put a limit on the number of pilgrims that will come from certain poor countries, but remove the limit for pilgrims that come from rich countries like America and Britain, have you done justly? Do you think God does not see? Yes, I want you to come to Christ because it is he alone that can deliver you from such bondage and evil, but your dissimulation now is ungodly.

The so-called "Protestant" and Evangelical movement is the most deceived of all the world religions. At least the others know that they are not Christians. The Protestant Reformation was begun by wealthy Germanic landlords who *protested* the Kaiser for preventing them from removing serfs from their land. These serfs had lived on them for hundreds of years. The Kaiser had received instruction from the Pope of Rome not to evict the poor. Coincidentally, Martin Luther was having an internal theological quarrel with the hierarchy of the Roman church at the same time. It was these rich German Landlords that joined Luther and offered him protection from the Pope, encouraging him to begin a new Church. Simultaneously King Henry VIII of England was having his troubles with the Pope over his insistence of marrying a third or fourth wife; I lost count. When he did not have his way, he started the Church of England. In the United States, it is called the Episcopal church.

I had earlier spoken about Judaism and other religions, but I will reiterate here that it is not a biblically-based religion. Just like the Catholic and Protestant religions that renamed their old gods with Christian names, the Judaic religion is a Babylonian-Persian religion that assumed the names and some of the traditions of the bible and bible heroes. For example, in the bible, the Hebrew New Year is observed around the "17th Month of Abib", which is sometime around April. However, Judaism observes its New Year between September and October. Secondly, and most profoundly, Hebrew tradition, like most other African cultures, delineates ancestry on the patrilineal basis, but Judaism does so on a matrilineal basis. While people can choose whatever religion they want, our contention with Judaism is that it is presented as the original Hebrew faith of the scriptures, which obviously it is not, which is leading many sincere worshippers toward destruction, just like the other religions we have before mentioned.

Someone might consider this message a bit tough, or as most say these days, "intolerant." However, if it causes one reader to re-examine her spiritual life, then it has been worth it.

THE WILDERNESS

NOW WE MOVE ON TO THE STRUGGLE TO ESCAPE EGYPT, AND some of Moses' personal shortcomings as he led the people out.

As many Bible readers know, God sent about ten plagues to Egypt, which he knew would not convince Pharaoh to set the people free. He knew that only the death of the First Born could set the people of Israel free, which was symbolic of the death of God's First Born Jesus. The Lambs that were killed by the Israelites that same night was symbolic of Jesus dying for our sins, and delivering us from sin, Egypt serving as a typology for Sin:

> *He is despised and rejected of men; a man of sorrows, and acquainted with grief: and we hid as it were our faces from him; he was despised, and we esteemed him not. Surely he hath borne our griefs, and carried our sorrows: yet we did esteem him stricken, smitten of God, and afflicted. But he was wounded for our transgressions, he was bruised for our iniquities: the chastisement of our peace was upon him; and with his stripes we are healed. All we like sheep have gone astray; we have turned every one to his own way; and the LORD hath laid on him the iniquity of us all. He was oppressed, and he was afflicted, yet he opened not his mouth: <u>he is brought as a lamb to the slaughter, and as a sheep before her shearers is dumb, so he openeth not his mouth</u>. He was taken from prison and from judgment: and who shall declare his generation? for he was cut off out of the land of the living: for the transgression of my people was he stricken (Is. 53:5).*

This scripture was written approximately 600 years before the birth of Jesus Christ.

Even today, we have personal issues and problems that all our prayer and fasting do not solve. Still, if we will appreciate the significance of the blood of Jesus as the essence of the nature of God. Just as the Hebrews placed the blood of the Lambs on the Lintel of their doors, we, by understanding the value of the blood, will be amazed to find that those apparent strongholds were not as tough as we assumed them to be. The mind is the battleground. The Proverb says, *"as a man thinketh in his heart, so is he, Eat and drink, saith he to thee; but his heart is not with thee"* (Prov. 23:7). Sometimes you think you know what you want, but your actions suggest that your heart is someplace else, which is what the wilderness experience was like for the children of Israel. They all said they wanted to go to the promised land, but through their actions, we could tell that their hearts were still in Egypt.

I surmise that all these religions, political differences, and economic hardships are orchestrated by men, to control the mass of people for personal gain. That gain could be financial, political, or metaphysical. However, the weapons by which you will truly overcome them are spiritual and not physically, or by violent means, which doesn't mean that there isn't a time for physical self-defense." *Here is the patience of the saints: here are they that keep the commandments of God, and the faith of Jesus"* (Rev.14:12). However, do not doubt that the response of these men to our opposition to their deeds will be physical violence. The Overcomers will have to resist with patience:

> *For we wrestle not against flesh and blood, but against principalities, against powers, against the rulers of the darkness of this world, against spiritual wickedness in high places. Wherefore take unto you the whole armour of God, that ye may be able to withstand in the evil day, and having done all, to stand* (Eph. 6:12-13).

Borrowing an analogy from the *Powel Doctrine* (Former US General), the Elect must be prepared to fight for the Kingdom on two fronts, with overwhelming spiritual force. The first battlefront is within us, and the second is the minds of other men.

Just as Moses and the children of Israel had to fight "Seven Abominable Nations," so it is now that we must fight many battles to purify ourselves, we must make no compromise with the world. We must show no mercy to any negativity within our hearts, such as jealousy, implacability, pride, self-centeredness, debauchery, etc.:

> *When the LORD thy God shall bring thee into the land whither thou goest to possess it, and hath cast out many nations before thee, the Hittites, and the Girgashites, and the Amorites, and the Canaanites, and the Perizzites, and the Hivites, and the Jebusites, seven nations greater and mightier than thou; And when the LORD thy God shall deliver them before thee; thou shalt smite them, and utterly destroy them; thou shalt make no covenant with them, nor shew mercy unto them* (Deut. 7:1).

We must overcome traits like Envy, Lust, and Pride. The seven nations spoken about in Deuteronomy are symbolic of these negative traits in us. Suppressing and overcoming these will put us in a position to be worthy witnesses of the Truth and empower us to stand boldly to propagate this message. While we fight the battle within, we should not stand idly by and be silent in the face of oppression of the poor and uninformed without.

The early Apostles were simple fishermen and tradesmen, but their association with Jesus caused them to turn the world upside down:

> *But the Jews which believed not, moved with envy, took unto them certain lewd fellows of the baser sort, and gathered a company, and set all the city on an uproar, and assaulted the house of Jason, and sought to bring them out to the people. And when they found them not, they drew Jason and certain brethren unto the rulers of the city, crying, These that have turned the world upside down are come hither also; Whom Jason hath received: and these all do contrary to the decrees of Caesar, saying that there is another king, one Jesus* (Acts 17:6).

When the children of Israel began their journey into the Promised Land, it was a journey slated to last 40 days. However, due to spiritual affliction and rebellion, it took them forty years, and none of the adults above twenty years of age from Egypt were found worthy to enter the Promised Land, not even Moses. The people grumbled too much, and Moses often did not follow the precise instructions of God, right from the days in which he confronted the Pharaoh.

This section of their journey has esoteric symbolism for us: our life is like the journey in the wilderness. Our attitude is often like the experience of the Children of Israel in the wilderness. Our temptations are often like the seven abominable nations. Sadly, just like many of the Israelites died in the wilderness, many of the believers shall not make it into the Kingdom. It is important always to make a distinction between Heaven and The Kingdom of Heaven (1 Corinthians 3:13-15). At the beginning of the book, we told you that YOU in a transformed state of being IS the Kingdom of God. Heaven is a place or state that you and I should already be in if we have come to believe the Testimony of God concerning Christ. *"And hath raised us up together, <u>and made us sit together in heavenly places in Christ Jesus</u>: That in the ages to come he might shew the exceeding riches of his grace in his kindness toward us through Christ Jesus"* (Eph. 2:6-7).

In the wilderness, just as Noah had built an Ark that had three levels, so also God commanded Moses to build a Tabernacle that had three Courts. These were called

"The Outer Court," "The Holy Place," and "The Holy of Holies." Within this structure were seven articles of service. These were the "Brazen Altar," "Brazen Laver," "Table of Shewbread," "Seven Golden Lampstands," "Altar of Incense," "Mercy Seat," and "Ark of Covenant" (see Figure 10). At this point, the reader should get a copy of the bible and study the following three chapters of Exodus to understand what we are about to discuss. (Ex. 25, 26, 30).

Much later, when Solomon had come into reign as King, he also was commissioned by God to build a Temple that was to hold those items from Moses' Tabernacle. These physical structures were to serve as a foreshadowing until the coming of the Messiah. With the coming of the Messiah, there is no longer a need for a physical building, and there will never be. Today people visit a location in Jerusalem, which they, unfortunately, believe to be the remnants of that Temple; however, it is not because the Romans destroyed the Temple in about AD 70 during the destruction of Jerusalem. The place known today as "the wailing wall" is the remnant of a Roman Army Garrison and contains nothing from Herod or Solomon's Temple.

And as he went out of the temple, one of his disciples saith unto him, Master, see what manner of stones and what buildings are here! And Jesus answering said unto him, Seest thou these great buildings? <u>there shall not be left one stone upon another</u>, that shall not be thrown down (Mk. 13:1-2).

1 Brazen Altar
2 Brazen Laver
3 Table of Shew Bread
4 Golden Censor
5 Golden Lampstand
6 Mercy Seat
7 Ark of the Covenant

Figure 10 – The Tabernacle of Moses

Sadly, the Christians, Jews, and Muslims continue to perpetuate the myth that the so-called "wailing wall" is the remnant of Herod's Temple.

The three courts in Noah's Ark, Moses Tabernacle, and Solomon's Temple are symbolic of the three aspects of Man: Spirit, Soul, and Body. The structure's seven items symbolize the stages of work to be done in the life of a person(s) who trusts in Christ. The first item being *the Brazen Altar*, symbolizing the place of Death to this world by the believer. The second, *the Brazen Laver*, symbolizes the work of cleansing done by the Word of God as represented by water, in the life of the believer. These first two are in the outer Court. The third, *the Table of Shewbread*, symbolizing the feasting on the Rhema Word of God daily by the believer. The fourth is *the Seven Golden Lampstands*, symbolic of the spiritual enlightenment that occurs in the life of the believer who has entered the Holy Place. The fifth item is *the Altar of Incense*, which symbolizes the acceptance of the believer's prayer, and the sanctification of it by Christ:

And another angel came and stood at the altar, having a golden censer; and there was given unto him much incense, that he should offer it with the prayers of all saints upon the golden altar which was before the throne. And the smoke of the incense, which came with the prayers of the saints, ascended up before God out of the angel's hand (Rev. 8:3-4).

The sixth item is *the Mercy Seat*, which entered the Holy Place *just once a year*, symbolizing the place of Jesus seated at the Right hand of God making intercession for the believer. "*Which he wrought in Christ, when he raised him from the dead, and set him at his own right hand in the heavenly places*" (Eph. 1:20). The seventh item was *the Ark of the Covenant*, made of wood, but overlaid with Gold, symbolizing the final overshadowing of humanity by the nature and presence of God. "*And when all things shall be subdued unto him, then shall the Son also himself be subject unto him that put all things under him, that God may be all in all*" (1 Cor. 15:28).

Now, just as Moses and his generation died in the wilderness, leaving Joshua his servant to carry the younger Israelites into the Promised land, so it is now. Christ commands us to lead the young toward the Kingdom, but many of us have lost our way. Sadly, those who have tied themselves into the Christian religion or the thing called "Christianity" are unable to enter the Kingdom because they think they have found the way. They are not able to see that it is *Baal* that they serve. They do not see the difference between being a Christian and following "Christianity", a Roman/ Mediterranean religion. These are well-meaning people who sometimes are actually "born again" and love Christ. However, a great veil is upon their minds as they study the Torah, The Tanakh, or the New Testament. It is those who understand the message we bring, that shall be found in the Kingdom. Without this understanding we cannot enter the Kingdom:

He answered and said unto them, Because it is given unto you to know the mysteries of the kingdom of heaven, <u>but to them it is not given</u>. For whosoever hath, to him shall be given, and he shall have more abundance: but whosoever hath not, from him shall be taken away even that he hath. Therefore speak I to them in parables: because they seeing see not; and hearing they hear not, neither do they understand (Matt. 13:11-13).

As it was then, so it is now.

Now, of course, everything in the Old Testament was symbolic of the real **Kingdom**, and not the very essence itself, for we know that Joshua died and left the people to settle in the land that he had conquered. They lived in a kind of loose confederacy and did what seemed right in their own eyes. "*In those days there was no king in Israel, but every man did that which was right in his own eyes*" (Judg. 17:6, Judg. 21:25). Even so, it is for us today. The LORD has not Returned yet, but the SAVIOR has come. In the interim, every one of us seems to be doing what appears to be right in our own eyes.

THE HOUSE OF DAVID

JUST AS JOSHUA DIED AND LEFT THE PEOPLE TO GOD AND THE ELDERS, so also did the early Apostles die and leave us in the hands of the Holy Spirit and the Christian elders. In consequence, just as the children of Israel rejected the Elders and Judges, demanding a King; we also have rejected the Holy Ghost and demanded Popes, Bishops, Pastors, Rabbis, Imams, etc. God wants us to trust in the blood and words of his Son, Jesus Christ. Not in men.

The prophet Samuel was the last of the elders and Judges that had tried to guide the people after Joshua had died. However, when the people saw the coordinated pomp and pageantry of their neighbors' kings, they demanded the same for themselves. Samuel tried to convince them that God was *their* King, but they insisted on getting a human being king like all the other nations. When God heard this, he told Samuel to give them what they asked. The first King was Saul, the son of Kish. He was tall and strong, and when the people saw him, they were excited and proud to have their King. However, Saul had a character flaw. He was insecure in himself. His first mistake was to feel outshone when God helped his son Johnathan gain victory over an enemy army. Saul, rather than celebrate the victory, commanded that no one should eat on that day.

The second mistake he made was an event where a foreign army besieged him. Each day as they prepared for battle, his soldiers became disillusioned and melted away from the battlefront at night. Now, according to custom, the King could not go into battle until the prophet came and offered a sacrifice to God (just like the Haitian general Dessalines waited for the priest *Dutty Boukman* about 200 years ago at the dawn of the Haitian revolution). However, because God delayed the prophet, the King became nervous and offered the sacrifice himself. He was not supposed to do that.

The third mistake was when he was called by God to go and destroy the Amalekites for something they had done 400 years earlier (God has a long memory), Saul did not do the job as directed by God through the Prophet. When confronted by the prophet on this matter, he lied and blamed it on his soldiers, and did not take responsibility as King. So, God rejected him.

Samuel also said unto Saul, The LORD sent me to anoint thee to be king over his people, over Israel: now therefore hearken thou unto the voice of the words of the LORD. Thus saith the LORD of hosts, I remember that which Amalek did to Israel, how he laid wait for him in the way, when he came up from Egypt. <u>Now go and smite Amalek, and utterly destroy all that they have, and spare them not</u>; but slay both man and woman, infant and suckling, ox and sheep, camel and ass. And Saul gathered the people together, and numbered them in Telaim, two hundred thousand footmen, and ten thousand men of Judah. And Saul came to a city of Amalek, and laid wait in the valley. And Saul said unto the Kenites, Go, depart, get you down from among the Amalekites, lest I destroy you with them: for ye shewed kindness to all the children of Israel, when they came up out of Egypt. So the Kenites departed from among the Amalekites. And Saul smote the Amalekites from Havilah until thou comest to Shur, that is over against Egypt. And he took Agag the king of the Amalekites alive, and utterly destroyed all the people with the edge of the sword. <u>But Saul and the people spared Agag, and the best of the sheep, and of the oxen, and of the fatlings, and the lambs, and all that was good, and would not utterly destroy them: but everything that was vile and refuse, that they destroyed utterly.</u> Then came the word of the LORD unto Samuel, saying, It repenteth me that I have set up Saul to be king: for he is turned back from following me, and hath not performed my commandments. And it grieved Samuel; and he cried unto the LORD all night. And when Samuel rose early to meet Saul in the morning, it was told Samuel, saying, Saul came to Carmel, and, behold, he set him up a place, and is gone about, and passed on, and gone down to Gilgal. And Samuel came to Saul: and Saul said unto him, Blessed be thou of the LORD: I have performed the commandment of the LORD. And Samuel said, What meaneth then this bleating of the sheep in mine ears, and the lowing of the oxen which I hear? And Saul said, They have brought them from the Amalekites: for the people spared the best of the sheep and of the oxen, to sacrifice unto the LORD thy God; and the rest we have utterly destroyed. Then Samuel said unto Saul, Stay, and I will tell thee what the LORD hath said to me this night. And he said unto him, Say on. And Samuel said, When thou wast little in thine own sight, wast thou not made the head of the tribes of Israel, and the LORD anointed thee king over Israel? And the LORD sent thee on a journey, and said, Go and utterly destroy the sinners the Amalekites, and fight against them until they be consumed. Wherefore then didst thou not obey the voice of the LORD, but didst fly upon the spoil, and didst evil in the sight of the LORD? And Saul said unto Samuel, Yea, I have obeyed the voice of the LORD, and *have gone the way which the LORD sent me, and have brought Agag the king of Amalek, and have utterly destroyed the Amalekites. <u>But the people took of the spoil, sheep and oxen, the chief of the things which should have been utterly destroyed, to sacrifice unto the LORD thy God</u> in Gilgal. And Samuel said, Hath the LORD as great delight in burnt offerings and sacrifices, as in obeying the voice of the LORD? Behold, <u>to obey is better than sacrifice, and to hearken than the fat of rams. For rebellion is as the sin of witchcraft, and stubbornness is as iniquity and idolatry. Because thou hast rejected the word of the LORD, he hath also rejected thee from being king.</u> And Saul said unto Samuel, I have sinned: for I have transgressed the commandment of the LORD, and thy words: because I feared the people, and obeyed their voice. Now therefore, I pray thee, pardon my sin, and turn again with me, that I may worship the LORD. And Samuel said unto Saul, I will not return with thee: for thou hast rejected the word of the LORD, and the LORD hath rejected thee from being king over Israel. And as Samuel turned about to go away, he laid hold upon the skirt of his mantle, and it rent. And Samuel said unto him, <u>The LORD hath rent the kingdom of Israel from thee this day, and hath given it to a neighbour of thine, that is better than thou.</u> And also the Strength of Israel will not lie nor repent: for he is not a man, that he should repent* (1 Sam. 15:1-26).

What moral lessons are there for us to learn from this about the children of Israel and their King? First, we should not seek any other King except the Son of God, Jesus Christ. Secondly, we do not need to be insecure and jealous of another person's success. Thirdly, we should not think of ourselves more highly than we ought to, and we should take responsibility for our mistakes and not blame it on others. Finally, it is vital to acknowledge that the "Amalekites" in our lives are not other people, but vices that we struggle against and must destroy. Religious activities cannot replace obedience to God. These are the traits of King Saul that can stop you and me from entering the Kingdom. David had flaws in nature, while Saul had flaws of Character.

Once the Spirit of God had departed from Saul, an evil demon would often come and torment him. His advisers suggested that he obtain a musician who could play the music that would soothe his soul. Coincidentally the young man David was a musician. The servants of the King found him and asked if he would like to be the musician of the King. He accepted the job. Every time the demon would come to disturb Saul, David would pick up his Harp and play the demon away. However, as time went on, Saul began to dislike David, and would often attempt to kill him. Fortunately, Johnathan, the son of Saul, loved David, and he protected David from King Saul.

When God saw that Saul was incorrigible, he commanded the prophet to anoint another king. This King was the boy David, the last of eight children:

> *Now David was the son of that Ephrathite of Bethlehem-Judah, whose name was Jesse;*
> *and he had eight sons: and the man went among men for an old man in the days of Saul.*
> *And the three eldest sons of Jesse went and followed Saul to the battle: and the names of his*
> *three sons that went to the battle were Eliab the firstborn, and next unto him Abinadab,*
> *and the third Shammah. And David was the youngest: and the three eldest followed Saul.*
> *But David went and returned from Saul to feed his father's sheep at Bethlehem* (1st. Sam
> 17:12-15).

The first book of Chronicles described David as the Seventh son (1st Chronicles 2:15). There is no mistake here. 1st Chronicles uses the chronological number of his birth position, while 1st Samuel uses the spiritual significance of 8 as it refers to a "New Beginning." David was the seventh son chronologically, But the Christ in him was the 8th Son spiritually. For example, in the new testament in the book of Matthew, we read:

> *So all the generations from Abraham to David are fourteen generations: and from David*
> *until the carrying away into Babylon are fourteen generations; and from the carrying away*
> *into Babylon unto Christ are fourteen generations (*Matthew 1:17).

There are thirteen generations from the carrying away into Babylon to Jesus, so Christ and his body are the fourteenth generation. You can see here that the fourteenth person is a spiritual being. The old testament uses the word "David" to describe Christ. The same spiritual person that took down Goliath. Isaiah refers to Christ as proceeding from Jesse: *"And there shall come forth a rod out of the stem of Jesse, and a Branch shall grow out of his roots"* (Isaiah 1:1). In the book of Revelations, Jesus refers to himself as the root and offspring of David: *"I Jesus have sent mine angel to testify unto you these things in the churches. I am the root and the offspring of David, and the bright and morning star "(Revelation 22:16).* We know Jesus had no earthly father, so how could he descend from Jesse or David? When did he descend from Jesse, was it 2000 years ago, or was it the night that Samuel showed up to anoint one of Jesse's sons as King? Since Christ pre-existed creation (Revelation 13:8), the eighth person referred to here is Christ.

A natural explanation of the discrepancy in numbering comes from the fact that in Israel if you had a brother that died without a child, you married his wife and dedicated that child to be the son of your brother in spirit and inheritance. So, if Jesse had a son for a deceased brother, he would count as his brother's son, not his own, according to custom. If you look back at our Table of Numbers, you will recall the number 8 signifies a new beginning.

Over time David found it necessary to flee into the wilderness and hide from King Saul. When it became too dangerous in the wilderness, he moved into the country of the Philistines as a refugee. Also, notice that David left King Saul's service when it was time for him to become King, and wandered into the camp of the Philistines, where he stayed for some time, even though they were enemies of Israel, so he did not belong there. So, it is today, that many of us have left the false churches in our hearts, but do not know what way to follow to reach the Kingdom. The Philistines were enemies of Israel and continually having skirmishes with them, but David never joined them to fight against Israel. He feigned madness. In the process of time, both Johnathan and Saul died in battle, but this saddened David rather than made him happy. He always honored Saul and felt it was not his place to judge Saul because God had anointed him king. As far as he was concerned, once God had anointed a man as King, no man could ever second guess God because God might be testing us. When he became King, he sought for any remaining children of Johnathan, Saul's surviving grandchildren, and made them sit with him in the Palace.

So, what moral lessons can we learn from the life of David as it relates to his attitude toward Saul and his family?

From the life of David, we can learn that the fact that we are going through tough times does not mean that God is unaware of our tribulations. Despite all the good that David brought to the life of King Saul by playing his Harp, he obtained no gratitude from him. There have been people you might have given the shirt on your back to, but their ingratitude and envy are so deep that they could never demonstrate humble appreciation. Eventually, those who choose to ignore the kindness they received will reap the fruit of their ingratitude. *"Whoso rewardeth evil for good, evil shall not depart from his house"* (Prov. 17:13).

Secondly, David never tried to defend himself by attacking his elder Saul. He left Saul to God and learned from Saul's mistakes. Once you have a certainty of yourself as a person of Destiny, you need not bother trying to win the acknowledgment of those invested in misrepresenting you. Over time, God will vindicate you because he chose you to be among the Elect.

Thirdly, God could have taken out Saul much earlier, but he chose to leave him on the throne for a long time to torment innocent David. He did this to teach us patience in the face of persecution, and fortitude, in the face of rejection.

The reign of Saul is symbolic of the time in which our spiritual life was "Carnal" and undeveloped. God chose us, but we did not have the experience and trial that time and difficulty can give. We claimed to know Christ, but, in our actions, we betrayed him. Like Saul, we carried jealousies and envy toward others and very little distinguished us from those on the outside. However, in all these things, God never left us because we had something that Saul never did, a mediator that God could not deny. The man Christ Jesus. *"For there is one God, and one mediator between God and men, the man Christ Jesus"* (1 Tim. 2:5).

During David's reign, he had sought to build a Temple for God, but because he had committed adultery and murder by sleeping with another man's wife, and then killing him, God rejected his offer. In trying to hide his wicked deed, David had plotted to kill the man. However, he saw the wickedness of his way and asked God for forgiveness. God forgave him but said only Solomon, David's son, would be allowed to build him the Temple.

Solomon was the third king of Israel and the last to reign over a united kingdom. Financial prosperity and the growth of knowledge and wisdom blessed his reign. He was offered anything he wanted by God but chose to ask only for Wisdom. God gave him both wisdom and great wealth. However, he loved many foreign women and allowed them to worship their gods within his Kingdom. Their worship of other gods offended God, and so he decreed that after the reign of Solomon, he would divide Israel in two, which he did during the reign of Solomon's son, Rehoboam.

Solomon was the third of the Kings that God had chosen. Do you remember what the number three symbolizes in the bible? Completion! God was sending a hidden message to us: after the reign of Solomon, the completion of the experiment to have a worthy human Kingdom without Christ was over. The idiosyncrasies of the three kings should have persuaded the people of Israel that they were better off with God as King, and not men. However, they never were able to see the meaning of the events. Even the great Solomon was unable to approximate the majesty of the Glory of God as we can today. *"And yet I say unto you, that even Solomon in all his glory was not arrayed like one of these"* (Matt. 6:29).

Today, we can reflect on the flaws of these great men. However, their lives serve as an example to us about the pitfalls that accompany those who say they are "religious" but do not have a worthy mediator to advocate for them. These men had no advocate as we do. When we make the same mistakes they made, we can continue reigning because we have Christ Jesus as our savior if we acknowledge our faults.

> *If we say that we have fellowship with him, and walk-in darkness, we lie, and do not the truth: But if we walk in the light, as he is in the light, we have fellowship one with another, and the blood of Jesus Christ his Son cleanseth us from all sin. If we say that we have no sin, we deceive ourselves, and the truth is not in us. If we confess our sins, he is faithful and just to forgive us our sins, and to cleanse us from all unrighteousness. If we say that we have not sinned, we make him a liar, and his word is not in us* (1 Jn. 1:6-10).

Now, even though both Saul and David were sinners, David was able to obtain mercy and favor from God because he understood the loving and forgiving character of God and was self-reflective while Saul was unable. It was not that Saul's sins were any worse than David's. I can confidently say that according to how morality in the sight of man is measured, David was a worse sinner than Saul. The sins of murder and taking of another man's wife are two of the worst sins that a person can commit. However, David was able to reflect on his actions and see the error of his ways. This reflection, coupled with his experience of the mercy of God during his younger days of hardships, made him approach God for leniency, while Saul turned instead to the ghost of Samuel and Fortune Tellers.

> *Then said Saul unto his servants, Seek me a woman that hath a familiar spirit, that I may go to her, and inquire of her. And his servants said to him, Behold, there is a woman that hath a familiar spirit at Endor. And Saul disguised himself, and put on other raiment, and he went, and two men with him, and they came to the woman by night: and he said, I pray thee, divine unto me by the familiar spirit, and bring me him up, whom I shall name unto thee. And the woman said unto him, Behold, thou knowest what Saul hath done, how he hath cut off those that have familiar spirits, and the wizards, out of the land: wherefore then layest thou a snare for my life, to cause me to die? And Saul sware to her by the LORD, saying, As the LORD liveth, there shall no punishment happen to thee for this thing. Then said the woman, Whom shall I bring up unto thee? And he said, Bring me up Samuel. And when the woman saw Samuel, she cried with a loud voice: and the woman spake to Saul, saying, Why hast thou deceived me? for thou art Saul. And the king said unto her, Be not afraid: for what sawest thou? And the woman said unto Saul, I saw gods ascending out of the earth. And he said unto her, What form is he of? And she said, An old man cometh*

up; and he is covered with a mantle. And Saul perceived that it was Samuel, and he stooped with his face to the ground, and bowed himself. And Samuel said to Saul, Why hast thou disquieted me, to bring me up? And Saul answered, I am sore distressed; for the Philistines make war against me, and God is departed from me, and answereth me no more, neither by prophets, nor by dreams: therefore I have called thee, that thou mayest make known unto me what I shall do. Then said Samuel, Wherefore then dost thou ask of me, seeing the LORD is departed from thee, and is become thine enemy? And the LORD hath done to him, as he spake by me: for the LORD hath rent the kingdom out of thine hand, and given it to thy neighbour, even to David: Because thou obeyedst not the voice of the LORD, nor executedst his fierce wrath upon Amalek, therefore hath the LORD done this thing unto thee this day. Moreover the LORD will also deliver Israel with thee into the hand of the Philistines: and tomorrow shalt thou and thy sons be with me: the LORD also shall deliver the host of Israel into the hand of the Philistines (1 Sam. 28:7-19).

Many of us have become like Saul. We go to any place called a "church" in search of some miracle or another to deliver us from what we fear. These things have a price.

SIGNIFICANCE OF THE THREE KINGS

S AUL, DAVID, AND THEN *SOLOMON:* THESE THREE KINGS AND WHAT they symbolize spiritually are the three stages of development for the person who becomes enlightened in Christ. The first stage, as exemplified by the life of Saul, is the carnal life you have lived up until the moment that you found the path of Christ. Though you now have the Life of Christ, you still act primarily based on your base human attributes. Attributes such as fear, jealousy, envy, implacability, manipulation, slander, greed, and other vices. You seek to get rid of these negative attributes, but do not understand how to.

The second stage is like the first, but it has one significant difference. The person at the second stage has all or some of these attributes in her life, but she is unhappy with these things, seeks to get rid of these vices, and is confident that Christ will eventually do the job. She cries to God for deliverance from these and is often self-reflective about her life. She obtains peace from knowing that God is a loving and forgiving God, and he will not allow her to suffer the evil conscience for longer than she can bear. This person is spiritual, while the first is carnal.

> *I have set the LORD always before me: because he is at my right hand, I shall not be moved. Therefore my heart is glad, and my glory rejoiceth: my flesh also shall rest in hope. For thou wilt not leave my soul in hell; neither wilt thou suffer thine Holy One to see corruption* (Ps. 16:8-10).

The third stage is one in which the person attains enlightenment, just as King Solomon did immediately, he sat on the throne. He received Wisdom. This wisdom of Christ is not like human wisdom in which we learn from experience. It is a wisdom in which our very essence and genetic structure, function in the reverence of the person of

God, and we flow with him unconsciously. A person in this stage moves about with a sort of glory invisible to the human eyes. They radiate authority and confidence that is often tempered by an inner humility. This third stage is where any person sincerely in search of the Kingdom would be. It is only a person in this third stage that is on the highway to the Kingdom. That is not to say those in the first two stages are not Saved. God reserves The Kingdom for those who are both Saved and chosen. Always remember, there is s difference between being "Saved," and being "Chosen." Only the Elect are chosen. All other believers are Saved:

> *They went out from us, but they were not of us; for if they had been of us, they would no doubt have continued with us: but they went out, that they might be made manifest that they were not all of us* (1 Jn. 2:19).

Only those in the third stage of growth can experience this glory.

THE TWO KINGDOMS

REHOBOAM WAS THE FOURTH KING. HE WAS THE SON OF Solomon, and it was during his reign that the Kingdom experienced a dividing. The people of Israel had come to him under the leadership of an exile named Jeroboam. This Jeroboam had been sought by King Solomon for treason and had fled to a foreign land. At the death of Solomon, he had returned from exile to plead with Rehoboam for forgiveness. Others had joined him to present their causes also.

King Rehoboam took counsel with the older men who had served under his father to see what their opinion was about this. They gave him good advice, saying he should welcome them and win them over. However, when he conferred with his young friends regarding what the older counselors had said, they told him to ignore the older men's advice. Instead, his friends advised him to tell Jeroboam and the people of Israel that came to plead that he would be even harsher than his father, Solomon. Rehoboam's discounting the advice of the older men who served under his wise father became his undoing and the catalyst for the rebellion of Jeroboam and ten of the twelve tribes against Rehoboam. There was a prophecy of something like this before the time of Rehoboam. So, in some ways, it was destined to happen:

> And the LORD was angry with Solomon, because his heart was turned from the LORD God of Israel, which had appeared unto him twice, And had commanded him concerning this thing, that he should not go after other gods: but he kept not that which the LORD commanded. Wherefore the LORD said unto Solomon, Forasmuch as this is done of thee, and thou hast not kept my covenant and my statutes, which I have commanded thee, I will surely rend the kingdom from thee, and will give it to thy servant. Notwithstanding in thy days I will not do it for David thy father's sake: but I will rend it out of the hand of thy son. Howbeit I will not rend away all the kingdom; but will give one tribe to thy son for David my servant's sake, and for Jerusalem's sake which I have chosen (1 Kings 11:9-13).

The only two tribes that remained with Rehoboam were Judah, his tribe, and Benjamin, the tribe of Saul. The other ten tribes broke off and named their nation Israel, while the kingdom under Rehoboam was called Judah. Over time God would send prophets and holy men and women to both nations to try to restore them to the path of pure and unadulterated worship of God, but he would be unsuccessful. Eventually, he would dissolve both kingdoms entirely through exile into Babylon and Persia.

Jeroboam was unsure of himself. He seemed always to doubt his legitimacy even though God had been the one to send a Prophet to anoint him King of the ten tribes.

> *And Jeroboam said in his heart, Now shall the kingdom return to the house of David: If this people go up to do sacrifice in the house of the LORD at Jerusalem, then shall the heart of this people turn again unto their lord, even unto Rehoboam king of Judah, and they shall kill me, and go again to Rehoboam king of Judah. Whereupon the king took counsel, and made two calves of gold, and said unto them, It is too much for you to go up to Jerusalem: behold thy gods, O Israel, which brought thee up out of the land of Egypt. And he set the one in Bethel, and the other put he in Dan. And this thing became a sin: for the people went to worship before the one, even unto Dan. And he made an house of high places, and made priests of the lowest of the people, which were not of the sons of Levi. And Jeroboam ordained a feast in the eighth month, on the fifteenth day of the month, like unto the feast that is in Judah, and he offered upon the altar. So did he in Bethel, sacrificing unto the calves that he had made: and he placed in Bethel the priests of the high places which he had made. <u>So he offered upon the altar which he had made in Bethel the fifteenth day of the eighth month, even in the month which he had devised of his own heart;</u> and ordained a feast unto the children of Israel: and he offered upon the altar, and burnt incense"* (1 Kings 11:26-33).

To secure his position, he built a fake altar and put up an effigy claiming that it was symbolic of God and that the ten tribes no longer needed to go down to Jerusalem to worship once a year as commanded by God. He did this because he felt the people would see Jerusalem and turn in their hearts to Judah. Many of the denominations today behave this way. Not wanting the believer to be free in Christ, peradventure, she does not return to that denomination, even if she has become a better Christian.

What can we learn from this phase of the development of Israel? First, the fact that listening to the wrong counselors can alter your life negatively. Had Rehoboam listened to the voice of the older men who had served under his father, he might have been able to delay the prophecy, or even change it. It is the same condition for the believer in Christ.

When he ascended, he sent the Holy Spirit to be our counselor. However, we accept more advice from psychologists and sociologists than we take from the Holy Ghost. We should not doubt that if we continue in this path, we will meet with the fortune of Israel and Judah in our personal lives.

> *And thou, even thyself, shalt discontinue from thine heritage that I gave thee; and I will cause thee to serve thine enemies in the land which thou knowest not: for ye have kindled a fire in mine anger, which shall burn for ever. Thus saith the LORD; Cursed be the man that trusteth in man, and maketh flesh his arm, and whose heart departeth from the LORD. For he shall be like the heath in the desert, and shall not see when good cometh; but shall inhabit the parched places in the wilderness, in a salt land and not inhabited* (Jer. 17:4-6).

Secondly, just like Israel and Judah became divided, and could never come together again, so it will be for those of us that choose to separate ourselves from the reproach of the gospel to another gospel that promises us pleasures in this life. Israel created a new place of worship for themselves on a mountain top and no longer went to Jerusalem to pray as God had commanded David and Solomon. Over time they no longer were sure whether praying in Jerusalem was a priority or on the mountain. For this reason, by the time of Jesus, we see the "Woman at the well" saying to him that he should worship on this mountain and not in Jerusalem:

> *Our fathers worshipped in this mountain; and ye say, that in Jerusalem is the place where men ought to worship. Jesus saith unto her, Woman, believe me, the hour cometh, when ye shall neither in this mountain, nor yet at Jerusalem, worship the Father* (Jn. 4:20-21).

Those who choose to determine their morality according to their fleshly desires will continue to call upon the name of the Lord, but they will never have that absolute certainty that they are in the will of God. They will preach a gospel, but it will always be "another gospel" and not "The gospel." They will seem to themselves and others as very pious and righteous but they will have been building a skyscraper of wood and hay. "*I marvel that ye are so soon removed from him that called you into the grace of Christ unto another gospel: Which is not another; but there be some that trouble you, and would pervert the gospel of Christ* "(Gal. 1:6-7).

Rehoboam, by not heeding the advice of the older men, and in our case, not heeding the Holy Ghost, we, just as the children of Israel, have entered a state of bewilderment.

We are unable to appropriate the "full counsel of God." Instead, we see little snippets of truth here and there, but we are unable to see the full picture of the message of Christ. For some, it is the message of "Prosperity," in which God is made akin to a lottery machine with whom we invest our hard-earned money, in the hope that he would one day multiply it. Contrary to the request by Jesus that we give expecting nothing in return. For others, it is "Faith to move mountains," even though the Holy Ghost tells us that even with great faith if we do not have love, we are nothing but loud-sounding empty gongs. For yet others, it is "Divine healing," even though we should realize that no matter how many times we are healed or raised from the dead, we shall all die one day if the Lord does tarry.

As stated at the beginning, the purpose of this book is to bring all people from whatever religion you are in, be it Islam, Hinduism, Christianity, Judaism, Taoism, etc. into a certainty of the power of faith in God through the person of Jesus Christ. The evidence is not found just in what we say. The counsel you receive directly from the Great God himself contains the proof of our authenticity. Your only obligation is to ASK him with your mouth. There is no demand from us that you join any Church or denomination. The only demand is that you ASK God if these things are correct. Is that a difficult thing to do? Certainly not. If it was difficult, you might have been more inclined to believe it.

So soon after the Apostles died, we can learn from history that the believers in Christ began to break up into little factions, just as natural Israel did under Rehoboam. That same pattern of dissolution sometimes occurs in the life of an individual after she has come to a personal revelation of the saving power of the Christ. She knows that something new and transformative has taken place in her life but soon is confronted with a demand for joining some denominational construct or another. She is moved from the simplicity of Faith she first had when she knew nothing about the different doctrines of the denominations. However, desiring to belong, she sets camp with one of the denominations, and so her downward spiral away from Christ begins. She is now a "Church Member." The glory departs. *"Woe unto you, scribes and Pharisees, hypocrites! for ye compass sea and land to make one proselyte, and when he is made, ye make him twofold more the child of hell than yourselves"* (Matt. 23:15). When you decide for Christ, do not emulate such a pattern. Instead, seek out small groups of men and women who want to pray and study together, even as they obey God in their personal lives.

Many denominations have sprouted up in the last two thousand years. Originally there was none. The first Apostasy was the Orthodox church headquartered in Turkey. A

Roman Emperor named Constantine instituted the church. Possibly there was an earlier apostasy in Ethiopia and Egypt in the early centuries CE, but our research has not been able to confirm this yet. There were Christians in Egypt and East Africa before the founding of the church of Constantine. Out of the Orthodox church came the Catholic church. Its break away from the Orthodox church occurred in 1054. An event often referred to as the *Great Schism*.

Other popular apostasies that have occurred include the so-called "Protestant Reformation." These movements, such as the Calvinist, Lutheran, Anglican, etc. are still considered by many to have been genuine attempts by well-meaning individuals to return the Christian church to the simplicity of the time of the first Apostles. However, there is no evidence of this in the actions of the prime leaders of these movements. Some of these leaders were Martin Luther, John Calvin, and even King Henry VIII of England, who began a new church because the Pope of Rome would not allow him to divorce his third wife.

In more recent times, we have had the Baptists, Seventh Day Adventists, Mennonites, and to some degree, the Pentecostal movement, all come out to announce themselves as the true path to Christ. Indeed, all these denominations and groups have some degree of knowledge and truth concerning Christ. Yet, none of them has adequately met the demand for simplicity, as advocated by the Apostles. By this we mean, each soul that comes to an understanding and faith in God through Christ, must be allowed to develop according to the leading of the Spirit of Christ in them, with only consultative support from other more experienced believers. Statements such as "WE BELIVE this, or WE BELIEVE that" should be reserved for those things explicitly stated in the New Testament scriptures.

We have taken time to elaborate on the preceding because the relationship of the individual with Christ rests on her assurance that she has a one on one communication with a living being who controls the universe. Any attempt to create an intermediary outside of Christ is an Apostasy:

> *Moreover I call God for a record upon my soul, that to spare you I came not as yet unto Corinth. <u>Not for that we have dominion over your faith,</u> but are helpers of your joy: for by faith ye stand* (2 Cor. 1:24).

The moral and spiritual messages that God would have us learn from this phase in the history of Israel is that lack of self-confidence will lead to idolatry. When you are not sure that you can open your mouth and pray, with the expectation that things will happen or that God will hear you, then you are tempted to turn to some man or woman to act as your intermediary. You suspend your rational mind and become a candidate for delusion and mind control. After a while, you will be unable to distinguish between Christ and Baal. *"And Elijah came unto all the people, and said, How long halt ye between two opinions? if the LORD be God, follow him: but if Baal, then follow him. And the people answered him not a word"* (1 Kings 18:21).

Just as the bible says that Jeroboam created his Priests from any tribe and his Feasts in the 8th month, so these denominations also created strange feast days that are supposed to represent events related to Christ or his Apostles. A command that he never gave. The only command he gave us was to love our neighbors.

Even now, there is the "true church," an entity we cannot see with the human eyes. Both we and those who have died physically are members together of this church:

> *And I John saw these things, and heard them. And when I had heard and seen, I fell down to worship before the feet of the angel which shewed me these things. Then saith he unto me, See thou do it not: for I am thy fellow servant, and of thy brethren the prophets, and of them which keep the sayings of this book: worship God* (Rev. 22:8-9).

There is also the false church. It is every denomination on earth. It is not purposely false. It is false because it is not the heavenly church that influences our hearts. The true church of Christ is heavenly, and those of us who are a part of it, have a love for one another, and all humankind. We are uncomfortable with backbiting and hurting each other. When we find ourselves doing any such thing, we feel terrible. We do not feel at ease with judging people based on their ethnicity etc. We always want to please the father. We seek to outdo one another in good deeds toward others. We love to study the word of God often. We do not have an inordinate desire for wealth or fame. We do not desire to rule over anyone. We are incredibly comfortable in our skins. We love to give honor to whom it is due. We show gratitude for the small things people do for us. We have peace and joy that is unexplainable. There are always unseen forces working for our good, even in the seemingly worst circumstances. A kind of serendipity always accompanies us:

> *The LORD is my shepherd; I shall not want. He maketh me to lie down in green pastures: he leadeth me beside the still waters. He restoreth my soul: he leadeth me in the paths of righteousness for his name's sake. Yea, though I walk through the valley of the shadow of*

death, I will fear no evil: for thou art with me; thy rod and thy staff they comfort me. Thou preparest a table before me in the presence of mine enemies: thou anointest my head with oil; my cup runneth over. Surely goodness and mercy shall follow me all the days of my life: and I will dwell in the house of the LORD forever (Psalm 23:1-6).

The era of the two Kingdoms ends with the eventual captivity of Israel and Judah and their exile into Babylon. However, before that would happen, God would send them Prophets to warn them.

THE PROPHETS

MANY OF THE PROPHETS ARE KNOWN AND BELIEVED AMONG adherents of the three major monotheistic religions. Elijah, Elisha, Jeremiah, Isaiah, Ezekiel, Jonah, etc. What is not known by most of these adherents is that all these prophets were pre-figures of Jesus Christ. You can look at several events in the lives of these men and see that they were a foreshadowing of Jesus. Let us look at some of these.

God sent Elijah to a widow in Zarephath. She was not an Israelite. There was hunger throughout Israel, but God did not choose to send Elijah to an Israelite widow. He selected the Gentile woman. He did this as an indication of how, in the future, he would choose the Gentiles over natural Israel to receive the mercy of God. How do we know this to be true? Jesus himself said so while discussing this event with the Judaic:

> But I tell you of a truth, many widows were in Israel in the days of Elias, when the heaven was shut up three years and six months, when great famine was throughout all the land; But unto none of them was Elias sent, save unto Sarepta, a city of Sidon, unto a woman that was a widow. And many lepers were in Israel in the time of Eliseus the prophet; and none of them was cleansed, saving Naaman the Syrian (Lk. 4:25-27).

God also showed the typology of Jesus in Elisha's ministry. When the sons of the prophets lost their iron ax-head in the waters, they called to Elisha for help. He took a piece of dry wood and threw it into the river, and surprisingly the iron ax-head came floating up while the wood descended. This miracle was a foreshadowing of how Jesus (Wood) would go down into Hell for us who were laden with sin (Iron) and bring us up from the grave. Not just the grave of physical death, but the grave of spiritual death:

> And one said, Be content, I pray thee, and go with thy servants. And he answered, I will go. So he went with them. And when they came to Jordan, they cut down wood. But as one

was felling a beam, the axe head fell into the water: and he cried, and said, Alas, master! for it was borrowed. And the man of God said, Where fell it? And he shewed him the place. And he cut down a stick, and cast it in thither; and the iron did swim. Therefore said he, Take it up to thee. And he put out his hand, and took it (2 Kings 6:3-7).

Jesus also reminded the people about how God used Elisha to heal Naaman the Leper from Syria, but not any Leper in Israel.

The prophet Jeremiah himself has an experience where the Generals of the King threw him into a dry well as punishment for prophesying that God would send Babylon to conquer Judah. However, when the Generals had gone to fight, the King sent his servant with THIRTY men to pull Jeremiah out of the well, and demanded that he meet him at the THIRD entrance of the Temple (Jer. 38:14). Concerning the number THIRTY, remember when we studied the numeric of God, we said, sometimes, when we multiply the single-digit by tens, hundreds, or thousands, it signifies the same meaning but in a more significant way. This story of Jeremiah is a foreshadowing of Jesus raised from the grave on the THIRD day.

Jonah's typology of Christ is a bit different because it refers to the resurrection of the people of Christ more than that of Jesus Christ himself. Jesus had the THIRD-day resurrection, but his people will attain the FOURTH-day resurrection. We have partaken in the THIRD-day resurrection in Jesus. God invites us to participate in the FOURTH-day resurrection of the Elect (The Son of Man). This typology is evident in the fact that Jonah was in the belly of the whale for three days AND three nights, and his coming out of the Whale on the FOURTH day is symbolic of the event that will happen regarding the *Sons of God* soon: the fourth-day resurrection. Recall that Jesus was NOT in the grave for three days AND three nights. He was there for two days and two nights and rose on the THIRD DAY:

"Now the LORD had prepared a great fish to swallow up Jonah. And Jonah was in the belly of the fish <u>three days and three nights"</u> (Jon. 1:17) "And after three days and an half the Spirit of life from God entered <u>into them,</u> and they stood upon their feet; and great fear fell upon them which saw them" (Rev.11:11-12).

The relationship between Elijah and his servant minister, Elisha, was a typology of the relationship between Jesus and the Christians. When Elijah went up in the chariot, Elisha received a double portion of the power that Elijah had:

And it came to pass, when they were gone over, that Elijah said unto Elisha, Ask what I shall do for thee, before I be taken away from thee. And Elisha said, I pray thee, let a double portion of thy spirit be upon me. And he said, Thou hast asked a hard thing: nevertheless, if thou see me when I am taken from thee, it shall be so unto thee; but if not, it shall not be so. And it came to pass, as they still went on, and talked, that, behold, there appeared a chariot of fire, and horses of fire, and parted them both asunder; and Elijah went up by a whirlwind into heaven. And Elisha saw it, and he cried, My father, my father, the chariot of Israel, and the horsemen thereof. And he saw him no more: and he took hold of his own clothes, and rent them in two pieces. He took up also the mantle of Elijah that fell from him, and went back, and stood by the bank of Jordan; And he took the mantle of Elijah that fell from him, and smote the waters, and said, Where is the LORD God of Elijah? and when he also had smitten the waters, they parted hither and thither: and Elisha went over (2 Kg. 2:9-14).

Jesus himself said that the Christians would exercise more power than him when he ascended. *"Verily, verily, I say unto you, He that believeth on me, the works that I do shall he do also; and greater works than these shall he do; because I go unto my Father"* (Jn. 14:12). To prove it, the Holy Ghost would heal people who simply were under the shadows of the Apostles, just like a dead man came alive after accidentally being dropped on Elisha's grave.

THE CAPTIVITY

MANY OTHER KINGS CAME AFTER BOTH REHOBOAM AND Jeroboam. Some were good, but most were evil. Israel seemed to have more bad Kings than Judah. The good Kings include Josiah, Asa, Hezekiah, Jotham, and Josaphat. The bad kings, about thirty-three in number, include Elah, Zimri, Ahizah, Ahab, the husband of Jezebel, and the strange Queen, Athaliah.

During the reign of these Kings, God often sent prophets to them and the people, warning them of catastrophe to come if they did not amend their ways. It is the same today. However, we seem to major on the minors, while the weightier issues regarding Love, Kindness, and Faith recede into the background. The believers often concentrate on things like paying tithes, or joining church committees, etc. as the more crucial issues to spend our time on. The loss of the physical Kingdom of Israel is nothing compared to the loss that awaits us if we fail to heed the warning of the Last Hour. We will not lose our salvation (If we trust in Christ), but we will lose our place in the kingdom:

> *Then saith he to his servants, The wedding is ready, but they which were bidden were not worthy. Go ye therefore into the highways, and as many as ye shall find, bid to the marriage. So those servants went out into the highways, and gathered together all as many as they found, both bad and good: and the wedding was furnished with guests. And when the king came in to see the guests, he saw there a man which had not on a wedding garment: And he saith unto him, Friend, how camest thou in hither not having a wedding garment? And he was speechless. Then said the king to the servants, Bind him hand and foot, and take him away, and cast him into outer darkness; there shall be weeping and gnashing of teeth. For many are called, but few are chosen* (Matt. 22:8-14).

Isaiah, Jeremiah, Ezekiel, Amos, Obadiah, Hosea, etc. are some of the prophets that God sent to try to warn the children of the two kingdoms, that they were going into captivity, but the people would not listen. Now we need to understand the esoteric meaning of captivity. For us, it does not mean that we will literally be taken to a foreign nation as happened to the Israelites. It means we shall be swept away by false teachings into a realm of spiritual alienation and incoherent doctrine. We shall seek to escape from darkness and enter into the Light of the kingdom but will be unable to until the time appointed for our captivity comes to an end. For many of us, that time has come, but for some of the readers, that time is still ahead. You are still struggling with the elementary principles of Christ, or you are still in one of the world's major religions, seeking Rest, but finding none.

The next segment of this chapter will quote extensively from the book of Daniel because the book gives details, through allegory concerning the nations and natures that shall dominate the earth and the world before the handing over of sovereignty to the Sons of God. The term used to describe these nations and natures is "Beasts" or "Creatures." While there are many biblical interpretations of exactly which beast corresponds to what nation in history, we will avoid that discussion for now. Instead, we will concentrate on the fact that AFTER the beasts have their time to rule on earth, the Sons of God, as typified by the allegorical "Son of Man" in Daniel Chapter seven, shall take over control of the earth and the world for Christ. Just as Daniel was captive, we also are in captivity now, waiting for the manifestation of the Sons of God to deliver us from the bondage of the current human nature, as well as the current socio-economic and political order. *"But ye are not in the flesh, but in the Spirit, if so be that the Spirit of God dwell in you. Now if any man have not the Spirit of Christ, he is none of his"* (Romans 8:9).

Our "captivity" is spiritual bondage perpetuated, paradoxically by the law of God itself, and our struggle to try to observe it binds us further in the net of sin:

> *Wherefore, my brethren, ye also are become dead to the law by the body of Christ; that ye should be married to another, even to him who is raised from the dead, that we should bring forth fruit unto God. For when we were in the flesh, the motions of sins, which were by the law, did work in our members to bring forth fruit unto death. But now we are delivered from the law, that being dead wherein we were held; that we should serve in newness of spirit, and not in the oldness of the letter. What shall we say then? Is the law sin? God forbid. Nay, I had not known sin, but by the law: for I had not known lust, except the law had said, Thou shalt not covet. But sin, taking occasion by the commandment, wrought in me all manner of concupiscence. For without the law sin was dead. For I was alive without the law once: but when the commandment came, sin revived, and I died. And the commandment, which was ordained to life, I found to be unto death. For sin, taking*

occasion by the commandment, deceived me, and by it slew me. Wherefore the law is holy, and the commandment holy, and just, and good. Was then that which is good made death unto me? God forbid. But sin, that it might appear sin, working death in me by that which is good; that sin by the commandment might become exceeding sinful. For we know that the law is spiritual: but I am carnal, sold under sin. For that which I do I allow not: for what I would, that do I not; but what I hate, that do I. If then I do that which I would not, I consent unto the law that it is good. Now then it is no more I that do it, but sin that dwelleth in me. For I know that in me (that is, in my flesh,) dwelleth no good thing: for to will is present with me; but how to perform that which is good I find not. For the good that I would I do not: but the evil which I would not, that I do. Now if I do that I would not, it is no more I that do it, but sin that dwelleth in me (Rom. 7:4-20).

We can see here that the Holy Ghost is warning those who have come to believe in Christ to be wary of the Law. He says that our nature is contrary to the Law, and as we keep attempting to live by the law, we continue to irritate the problem, which is our sinful nature. So those of us who have come into rest in Christ and observe the transformation taking place in our nature through the unobservable work of the Holy Spirit, are more easily able to fulfill the requirements of the Law. In contrast, people who are trying hard to satisfy the law's requirements by their knowledge of the Law are perpetuating their stay in captivity.

The period of the captivity of natural Israel was the era of Daniel, Ezra, Nehemiah, Esther, and Mordecai. Daniel had been taken captive as a young boy when Nebuchadnezzar had conquered Judah. Daniel received the most vivid vision of the kingdoms that would precede the coming Kingdom of God. He received five documented visions that have both natural and esoteric significance. We will study the first two. God willing, we will explore the others in future books.

Daniel two contains the first vision:

Thou, O king, sawest, and behold a great image. This great image, whose brightness was excellent, stood before thee; and the form thereof was terrible. This image's head was of fine gold, his breast and his arms of silver, his belly and his thighs of brass, His legs of iron, his feet part of iron and part of clay. Thou sawest till that a stone was cut out without hands, which smote the image upon his feet that were of iron and clay, and brake them to pieces. Then was the iron, the clay, the brass, the silver, and the gold, broken to pieces together, and became like the chaff of the summer threshing floors; and the wind carried them away, that no place was found for them: and the stone that smote the image became a great mountain, and filled the whole earth (Dan. 2:31-35).

The second is in Daniel seven:

And four great beasts came up from the sea, diverse one from another. The first was like a lion, and had eagle's wings: I beheld till the wings thereof were plucked, and it was lifted up from the earth, and made stand upon the feet as a man, and a man's heart was given to it. And behold another beast, a second, like to a bear, and it raised up itself on one side, and it had three ribs in the mouth of it between the teeth of it: and they said thus unto it, Arise, devour much flesh. After this I beheld, and lo another, like a leopard, which had upon the back of it four wings of a fowl; the beast had also four heads; and dominion was given to it. After this I saw in the night visions, and behold a fourth beast, dreadful and terrible, and strong exceedingly; and it had great iron teeth: it devoured and brake in pieces, and stamped the residue with the feet of it: and it was diverse from all the beasts that were before it; and it had ten horns. I considered the horns, and, behold, there came up among them another little horn, before whom there were three of the first horns plucked up by the roots: and, behold, in this horn were eyes like the eyes of man, and a mouth speaking great things. I beheld till the thrones were cast down, and the Ancient of days did sit, whose garment was white as snow, and the hair of his head like the pure wool: his throne was like the fiery flame, and his wheels as burning fire. A fiery stream issued and came forth from before him: thousand thousands ministered unto him, and ten thousand times ten thousand stood before him: the judgment was set, and the books were opened. I beheld then because of the voice of the great words which the horn spake: I beheld even till the beast was slain, and his body destroyed, and given to the burning flame. As concerning the rest of the beasts, they had their dominion taken away: yet their lives were prolonged for a season and time. I saw in the night visions, and, behold, one like the Son of man came with the clouds of heaven, and came to the Ancient of days, and they brought him near before him. And there was given him dominion, and glory, and a kingdom, that all people, nations, and languages, should serve him: his dominion is an everlasting dominion, which shall not pass away, and his kingdom that which shall not be destroyed (Dan. 7:3-14).

Daniel chapter eight contains the third vision:

Then I lifted up mine eyes, and saw, and, behold, there stood before the river a ram which had two horns: and the two horns were high; but one was higher than the other, and the higher came up last. I saw the ram pushing westward, and northward, and southward;

so that no beasts might stand before him, neither was there any that could deliver out of his hand; but he did according to his will, and became great. And as I was considering, behold, an he goat came from the west on the face of the whole earth, and touched not the ground: and the goat had a notable horn between his eyes. And he came to the ram that had two horns, which I had seen standing before the river, and ran unto him in the fury of his power. And I saw him come close unto the ram, and he was moved with choler against him, and smote the ram, and brake his two horns: and there was no power in the ram to stand before him, but he cast him down to the ground, and stamped upon him: and there was none that could deliver the ram out of his hand. Therefore the he goat waxed very great: and when he was strong, the great horn was broken; and for it came up four notable ones toward the four winds of heaven. And out of one of them came forth a little horn, which waxed exceeding great, toward the south, and toward the east, and toward the pleasant land. And it waxed great, even to the host of heaven; and it cast down some of the host and of the stars to the ground, and stamped upon them. Yea, he magnified himself even to the prince of the host, and by him the daily sacrifice was taken away, and the place of his sanctuary was cast down. And an host was given him against the daily sacrifice by reason of transgression, and it cast down the truth to the ground; and it practiced, and prospered. Then I heard one saint speaking, and another saint said unto that certain saint which spake, How long shall be the vision concerning the daily sacrifice, and the transgression of desolation, to give both the sanctuary and the host to be trodden under foot? And he said unto me, Unto two thousand and three hundred days; then shall the sanctuary be cleansed (Dan. 8:3-14).

Daniel chapter nine contains the fourth vision:

Yea, whiles I was speaking in prayer, even the man Gabriel, whom I had seen in the vision at the beginning, being caused to fly swiftly, touched me about the time of the evening oblation. And he informed me, and talked with me, and said, O Daniel, I am now come forth to give thee skill and understanding. At the beginning of thy supplications the commandment came forth, and I am come to shew thee; for thou art greatly beloved: therefore understand the matter, and consider the vision. Seventy weeks are determined upon thy people and upon thy holy city, to finish the transgression, and to make an end of sins, and to make reconciliation for iniquity, and to bring in everlasting righteousness, and to seal up the vision and prophecy, and to anoint the most Holy. Know therefore and understand, that from the going forth of the commandment to restore and to build Jerusalem unto the Messiah the Prince shall be seven weeks, and threescore and two weeks: the street shall be built again, and the wall, even in troublous times. And after threescore and two weeks shall Messiah be cut off, but not for himself: and the people of the prince that shall come shall destroy the city and the sanctuary; and the end thereof shall be with a flood, and unto the end of the war desolations are determined. And he shall confirm the covenant with many for one week: and in the midst of the week he shall cause the sacrifice and the oblation to cease, and for the overspreading of abominations he shall make it desolate, even until the consummation, and that determined shall be poured upon the desolate (Dan. 9:21-27).

The fifth and final vision extends from Chapters 10-12 (Dan. 10, 11, 12.). Please read these for yourself in a bible and return to this book. We will investigate the prophecies of Daniel and see what spiritual and esoteric messages we can obtain from them. The next chapter will concentrate on exposing the esoteric meanings of the first two visions.

THE VISIONS OF DANIEL

THE KING OF BABYLON, NEBUCHADNEZZAR, RECEIVED THE FIRST vision. The dream troubled him so much that he asked his fortune-tellers, not only to interpret the dream but first to tell him what he dreamt if they really were seers. Of course, they all said that it was impossible to give the interpretation if he did not tell them what he dreamt. The King was angry and put them all in jail until they could inform him what he dreamt. However, when Daniel heard about the king's anger and demand, he prayed to God and asked him to reveal not only what the King dreamt, but also the interpretation thereof.

King Nebuchadnezzar's dream was this; he saw a great image of some sort with a Gold head, Silver chest and arms, Bronze belly and thighs, Iron legs, but the feet were partly of Clay and in part of Silver. Daniel tells the king that the head of Gold represents the king, while the chest and arms of Silver represent another kingdom to arise after Babylon. Most bible scholars believe that the second Kingdom was the Persian, the third was the Greek, and the fourth was the Roman. While this might be correct, it is important to point out that, even though those empires ended, their spiritual influence continues even today. We can tell this by noticing them again in the book of Revelation, Chapter 13. The same four beasts from Daniel Chapters Seven and Eight are found in Revelation, Chapter 13. If the vision of them in Daniel referred only to past kingdoms, then we would not see them again in Revelation Chapter 13. While in one vision, Nebuchadnezzar saw them as different aspects of an image; Daniel Seven and Eight shows them as Four Beasts -Lion, Leopard, Bear, and a fourth indescribable beast with the horns of a Ram.

Furthermore, Daniel did not seem to declare the Kingdom of the feet a separate Kingdom from the kingdom of the legs. However, we can tell by the grace of the spirit of Christ that it is a different Kingdom but emanating from the Kingdom of Iron. The Kingdom of Iron was the Roman Empire. The Kingdom that was part of Iron and partly of Clay is the modern world system that has emanated from the vestiges of the Holy Roman Empire. No matter how remote a culture is from old Rome today, it is the Roman religious and political system that still dominates the world.

Our primary concern then should be the last kingdom with its feet of part Iron and Clay. Daniel also describes it as the fourth Beast, too enigmatic to describe, and that subdues the whole earth. Clay is dust, and dust is symbolic of the nature of man in scripture. Iron is symbolic of Sin. Is it a coincidence that the bible tells us in the New Testament that we are to expect a "man of sin" who will dominate the world?

> *Let no man deceive you by any means: for that day shall not come, except there come a falling away first, and that man of sin be revealed, the son of perdition; Who opposeth and exalteth himself above all that is called God, or that is worshipped; so that he as God sitteth in the temple of God, shewing himself that he is God (2. Thess. 2:3-4).*

It cannot be a contiguous nation because Daniel says, *"And whereas thou saw iron mixed with miry clay, they shall mingle themselves with the seed of men: but they shall not cleave one to another, even as iron is not mixed with clay"* (Dan. 2:45). This description is evidence that this is not a United Nation. Only in modern times have we first experimented with the concept of putting together very diverse peoples into one geographical space and calling them a nation. The first nation that ever attempted this was the Romans. That eventually led to their downfall. The same shall happen to all the nations of the earth today. The painful consequences can be minimized by understanding scripture and granting as much autonomy as possible to all the nations within countries today that are different in custom and tradition from each other:

> *And hath made of one blood all nations of men for to dwell on all the face of the earth, and hath determined the times before appointed, and the bounds of their habitation; That they should seek the Lord, if haply they might feel after him, and find him, though he be not far from every one of us: For in him we live, and move, and have our being; as certain also of your own poets have said, For we are also his offspring (Acts. 17:26).*

At the end of this vision, Nebuchadnezzar saw a stone cut out of a mountain without hands, and the stone was cast at the image and destroyed the Gold, Silver, Bronze, Iron, and Clay. The mountain is symbolic of Zion, the true believers in Christ, while the stone CUT OUT of the mountain represents THE ELECT of God chosen from out of the true church. It is these who will bring down the system of the world and establish the Kingdom of God on earth. The world's system is brought down by casting down the images that control the minds of men and women today on earth. *"Casting down imaginations, and every high thing that exalteth itself against the knowledge of God, and bringing into captivity every thought to the obedience of Christ"* (2 Cor. 10:5). The truth of the gospel of Christ, as spoken by the Holy Ghost, is what shall accomplish this.

The second vision concerns Daniel's seeing four beasts. The first beast was LIKE a Lion with Eagle's wings. The second beast was LIKE a Bear and had three ribs in its mouth. The third beast was LIKE a Leopard, having four heads and four wings of a fowl. Lastly, the fourth beast (indescribable) had TEN horns and destroyed all the others. But out from among the TEN horns came out a small horn that destroyed three of the other horns. It had the eyes of a man and spoke boastfully.

While Daniel was still looking, he saw the power of all these beasts cast down, and a person he refers to as "The Ancient of Days" sitting on a throne. While gazing at this wonder, he noticed a human being, being brought to the Ancient of Days to receive reward and honor. God gives the person the authority to rule over all of creation forever.

A bystander in the vision told Daniel that the four beasts represented the forces that currently dominate the world, (not to be confused with the four beasts of Ezekiel and Revelation Chapter 4). That at the end of time, THE PEOPLE OF GOD would overthrow those forces and establish a Kingdom of Righteousness on earth.

The great thing about this vision is that we do not need to speculate on what it means. God is kind enough to give us the interpretation right there. You and I will one day take over control of this world and rule it according to the righteous dictates of God. We are that "Son of Man" that is brought to the Ancient of Days to receive the authority:

> *But the judgment shall sit, and they shall take away his dominion, to consume and to destroy it unto the end. And the kingdom and dominion, and the greatness of the kingdom under the whole heaven, shall be given to the people of the saints of the most High, whose kingdom is an everlasting kingdom, and all dominions shall serve and obey him* (Dan. 7:26-27).

So, we can see from scripture what the intent of God is for us. He intends for those who follow Christ to be the rulers on earth someday. However, other dark forces must be allowed to test us and strengthen us. As this goes on, we not only get stronger, but like David, we learn not to rule like the forces that govern today. This testing all connects back to what we studied about the character of David, and that of King Saul. Through these tribulations, we are currently experiencing under the rule of the Beast; we are developing within ourselves patience, longsuffering, love, kindness, joy, and all other virtues that are synonymous with godliness.

There is a gentleness that God desires to nurture within us, through the tribulation that is to come upon the whole world. The intent of these present difficulties in our personal and national lives is to make us more sensitive to the sufferings of our neighbors. It is God's way of determining whether we will be faithful with immense power when the time comes. The book of Daniel shows us the arrogance of the beastly governments. The jockeying for power without care for the poor and needy. Daniel shows us clearly that this world system will come to an end. Not with the power of man, but by the divine intervention of God through men.

THE MINISTRY OF JESUS

JESUS WAS THE LAST OLD TESTAMENT PROPHET, EVEN THOUGH HE WAS more than a prophet. In the same sense that a homeowner is more important than the home itself. He came to fulfill the requirements of the Old Testament:

> *Think not that I am come to destroy the law, or the prophets: I am not come to destroy, but to fulfil. For verily I say unto you, Till heaven and earth pass, one jot or one tittle shall in no wise pass from the law, till all be fulfilled. Whosoever therefore shall break one of these least commandments, and shall teach men so, he shall be called the least in the kingdom of heaven: but whosoever shall do and teach them, the same shall be called great in the kingdom of heaven. For I say unto you, That except your righteousness shall exceed the righteousness of the scribes and Pharisees, ye shall in no case enter into the kingdom of heaven"* (Matt. 5:17-20).

Therefore, you would often see him make statements like "go not to the road of the Gentiles":

> *These twelve Jesus sent forth, and commanded them, saying, Go not into the way of the Gentiles, and into any city of the Samaritans enter ye not: But go rather to the lost sheep of the house of Israel* (Matt. 10:5-6).

The reason Jesus would tell his disciples not to go to the Gentiles was that the time for the Gentiles had not yet come. Natural Israel first had to reject him to fulfill the plan of and purposes of God for all mankind. Even when they would require him to pay the Temple tax, Jesus would oblige even though he knew that the ritual was obsolete. Even John the Baptist told him he did not need Baptism, but Jesus told him to go ahead and baptize him to fulfill all the requirements of the old testament. (I just love Jesus).

Most of us are familiar with his birth story, but certain aspects of it need revisiting for clarity. First, it is doubtful that he was born in December because the story tells us that the Shepherds were out in the field at night sleeping. Wintertime is not usually when Shepherds sleep in the open. Secondly, Magi from the East visit him. They brought with them gifts for the baby Jesus whom their astrological observations had determined would be born at that time. The scriptures tell us of three gifts, NOT three wise men. The gifts were Gold, Frankincense, and Myrrh. The esoteric meaning of Gold symbolized his Kingship over Israel, the Frankincense represented his Priestly role after the Order of Melchizedek, and the Myrrh represented his calling as a Prophet. Matthew, chapter two, contains this account.

King Herod, who was on the throne at the time of Jesus' birth, had intended to kill the baby Jesus when he discovered he had been born. Most of us do not fully appreciate why Herod felt a need to murder the child. He felt driven to murder the child based on a prophecy he believed. You see, Herod was a descendant of the Edomites. The Edomites were the children of Esau, Jacob's brother. Jacob, the ancestor of the Israelites, had stolen the Birthright from Esau as we read earlier. Isaac, their father, had promised a grieving Esau that a time would come when his descendants would wrestle back the authority from Jacob/Israel:

> And Isaac answered and said unto Esau, Behold, I have made him thy lord, and all his brethren have I given to him for servants; and with corn and wine have I sustained him: and what shall I do now unto thee, my son? And Esau said unto his father, Hast thou but one blessing, my father? bless me, even me also, O my father. And Esau lifted up his voice, and wept. And Isaac his father answered and said unto him, Behold, thy dwelling shall be the fatness of the earth, and of the dew of heaven from above; And by thy sword shalt thou live, and shalt serve thy brother; _and it shall come to pass when thou shalt have the dominion, that thou shalt break his yoke from off thy neck_ (Gen. 27:37-40).

Likewise, the Kingdom promise transferred from overly religious people who seek God's favor through observing church dogma to people with no prior knowledge of Christ who accept the simplicity of his gospel. The parable of the marriage feast articulates this transfer:

> Then said he unto him, A certain man made a great supper, and bade many: And sent his servant at supper time to say to them that were bidden, Come; for all things are now ready. And they all with one consent began to make excuse. The first said unto him, I have bought

a piece of ground, and I must needs go and see it: I pray thee have me excused. And another said, I have bought five yoke of oxen, and I go to prove them: I pray thee have me excused. And another said, I have married a wife, and therefore I cannot come. So that servant came, and shewed his lord these things. Then the master of the house being angry said to his servant, Go out quickly into the streets and lanes of the city, and bring in hither the poor, and the maimed, and the halt, and the blind. And the servant said, Lord, it is done as thou hast commanded, and yet there is room. And the lord said unto the servant, Go out into the highways and hedges, and compel them to come in, that my house may be filled. For I say unto you, That none of those men which were bidden shall taste of my supper (Lk. 14:16-24).

Many long-time believers "bidden" to the marriage feast of the Kingdom, opt for religion and dogma instead of the perpetual Grace of God. They do not understand that God calls us to a more significant promise just beyond salvation, which is a promise to enter the Kingdom of God. Esau did not lose his relationship with God; he lost his birthright.

Let us therefore fear, lest, a promise being left us of entering into his rest, any of you should seem to come short of it. For unto us was the gospel preached, as well as unto them: but the word preached did not profit them, not being mixed with faith in them that heard it (Heb. 4:1-2).

Christ's descent from both Abraham and David fulfills the promise that God made to both David and Abraham. This part of his story is crucial because, in the promises that God made to Abraham and David, he tells them that their sons, Isaac and Solomon would be the ones through whom he would fulfill his promises. However, the Apostles tell us that God does "not dwell in Temples made by hands."

Which also our fathers that came after brought in with Jesus into the possession of the Gentiles, whom God drave out before the face of our fathers, unto the days of David; Who found favour before God, and desired to find a tabernacle for the God of Jacob. But Solomon built him an house. Howbeit the most High dwelleth not in temples made with hands; as saith the prophet, Heaven is my throne, and earth is my footstool: what house will ye build me? saith the Lord: or what is the place of my rest? (Acts 7:45-49).

Therefore, we can confirm that the individual that God referred to, esoterically, when speaking to both Abraham and David, was not their natural heir, but one who was to come later, <u>Christ Jesus</u>:

> *Now to Abraham and his seed were the promises made. He saith not, And to seeds, as of many; but as of one, And to thy seed, which is Christ. And this I say, that the covenant, that was confirmed before of God in Christ, the law, which was four hundred and thirty years after, cannot disannul, that it should make the promise of none effect* (Gal. 3:16-17).

If you noticed, in the last paragraph, we used the name "Christ Jesus," and not Jesus Christ. Reading through the genealogy of Jesus found in the book of Matthew Chapter One, you will notice that even though it promises a genealogy of Fourteen generations from the "Captivity to Christ," it only gives us thirteen generations to "Jesus Christ." Is there an error in God's numeric? No. Jesus Christ is the Son of God who died for our sins, but Christ Jesus is the *Resurrected* Savior and us as his body. Jesus is the Head of that body. Christ Jesus is the power of God that flows through me and all who have come to put their trust in him. Jesus himself being the first to experience the power of The Resurrected Christ.

In Matthew's genealogical account, there were fourteen generations to *Christ*, but thirteen generations to *Jesus Christ*, the King of the Israelites who the people rebelled against and chose Barabbas as their hero instead. Remember number thirteen and its esoteric meaning? Remember that this is a deeper look at the spiritual messages contained within the scriptures. It is not a surface level teaching. Christ withheld it before now, but at this time is being revealed to us.

According to the book of John, the first miracle that Jesus performed was the changing of water into wine. It is noteworthy that he would use the changing of water into wine as his first act. The reason it is significant is because of its esoteric connotation. Water is symbolic of the "Word of God":

"That he might sanctify and <u>cleanse it with the washing of water by the word</u>, That he might present it to himself a glorious church, not having spot, or wrinkle, or any such thing; but that it should be holy and without blemish (Eph. 5:26-27).

To change it into wine connotes transformation of a simple Word into something more powerful when Jesus stimulates that word. Only he can take a seemingly powerless Word and transform it into a life-giving Spirit. God willing, he will do that in our lives each day we investigate his Word.

Now we enter the critical stage of his ministry. This stage is when for *three and a half years*, he traveled around the country preaching the message of the Kingdom of God. He tells the people and their leaders that we must fulfill the requirements of the law to enter the Kingdom of God. However, he makes it evident that since God is Spirit, his law is spiritual. For example, he says,

> *Ye have heard that it was said by them of old time, Thou shalt not commit adultery: But I say unto you, That whosoever looketh on a woman to lust after her hath committed adultery with her already in his heart* (Matt.5:27-28).

If the Law is spiritual, then natural (Carnal) man cannot fulfill it.

The theme of Jesus' message was that it was impossible to keep the requirements of the Law while in human flesh descended from Adam. He never told people NOT to keep the Law. He just kept on trying to demonstrate to them the impossibility of pleasing God by trying to keep the Law. Almost every altercation he had concerning the Laws was somehow within this context, even when they brought before him for Judgment, the woman "caught" in adultery. When pressed to give his verdict concerning her in comparison to what Moses had declared in the Law, he did not deny that they should stone her. He simply asked the person who was not guilty of a similar sin to cast the first stone. They all dropped their stones and walked away "from the eldest to the youngest."

Another aspect of Jesus revealed in the scripture was his eternal existence as a non-created being. Therefore, equating himself with Christ from birth. In fact, at one time he stated that:

> *Then said the Jews unto him, Thou art not yet fifty years old, and hast thou seen Abraham? Jesus said unto them, Verily, verily, I say unto you, <u>Before Abraham was, I am</u>. Then took they up stones to cast at him: but Jesus hid himself, and went out of the temple, going through the midst of them, and so passed by* (Jn.8:57-59).

This name I AM is a name used by God to declare himself to Moses in the Old Testament. There was no doubt in the ears of the hearers who Jesus was claiming to be. Also, in the book of Matthew, Jesus takes some of his disciples with him to a mountain alone. While they were there, Moses and Elijah appeared to Jesus, and his clothes became bright light. When the disciples saw this, they were astonished. The significance of this is that the two men represented "the Law and the Prophets." A common phrase used to distinguish the "Torah" from the "Tanakh." Their coming to Jesus meant that they recognized him as the special one, and they had come to get instructions from him about the future:

> And it came to pass about eight days after these sayings, he took Peter and John and James, and went up into a mountain to pray. And as he prayed, the fashion of his countenance was altered, and his raiment was white and glistering. And, behold, there talked with him two men, which were Moses and Elias: Who appeared in glory, and spake of his decease which he should accomplish at Jerusalem (Lk. 9:28-31).

Two major phenomena characterize Jesus' ministry: teaching and miracles. We already looked at some of his doctrine and a miracle. Let us look at a few more of his miracles and their significance. His doctrine will be better articulated when we get to the teaching of the Apostles.

One miracle Jesus did was the raising of Lazarus AFTER three days.

> Jesus therefore again groaning in himself cometh to the grave. It was a cave, and a stone lay upon it. Jesus said, Take ye away the stone. Martha, the sister of him that was dead, saith unto him, <u>Lord, by this time he stinketh: for he hath been dead four days</u>. Jesus saith unto her, Said I not unto thee, that, if thou wouldest believe, thou shouldest see the glory of God? Then they took away the stone from the place where the dead was laid. And Jesus lifted up his eyes, and said, Father, I thank thee that thou hast heard me. And I knew that thou hearest me always: but because of the people which stand by I said it, that they may believe that thou hast sent me. And when he thus had spoken, he cried with a loud voice, Lazarus, come forth. And he that was dead came forth, bound hand and foot with graveclothes: and his face was bound about with a napkin. Jesus saith unto them, Loose him, and let him go (Jn. 11:38-44).

What is significant about this is not just that he raised a dead man, but that he chose to do it on the FOURTH day. He had spoken earlier of the "sign of Jonah" being the raising of the "son of Man" AFTER three days:

> But he answered and said unto them, An evil and adulterous generation seeketh after a sign; and there shall no sign be given to it, but the sign of the prophet Jonas: For as Jonas was three days and three nights in the whale's belly; so shall the Son of man be three days and three nights in the heart of the earth (Matt. 12:39-40).

As we should know, Jesus himself rose from the dead on the THIRD day. So, who is this "Son of Man"? If you recall what we read about Daniel's vision in Chapter 7 of Daniel, you will find the answer. Why don't you flip back to that page and see what the prophet Daniel is told about who the Son of Man is?

So, the raising of Lazarus was symbolic of the raising of each person that will be found worthy to participate in the FOURTH DAY resurrection. This Fourth Day resurrection is "the better resurrection." This Resurrection is more than an event; it is a person:

> *Jesus said unto her, I am the resurrection, and the life: he that believeth in me, though he were dead, yet shall he live: And whosoever liveth and believeth in me shall never die. Believest thou this?* (Jn. 11:25-26).

Once a person takes part in the resurrection life, she attains some degree of the personality of Jesus. The fourth day is the day that God created the Sun, Moon, and Stars. The APOSTLE Paul tells us that the Resurrection shall be like the glory of the Sun, Moon, and Stars:

> *There is one glory of the sun, and another glory of the moon, and another glory of the stars: for one star differeth from another star in glory. <u>So also is the resurrection of the dead.</u> It is sown in corruption; it is raised in incorruption: It is sown in dishonour; it is raised in glory: it is sown in weakness; it is raised in power: It is sown a natural body; it is raised a spiritual body* (1 Cor. 15:41-44).

Another miracle of Jesus was that which he did at the pool of Bethsaida. The scriptures tell us that there was a man who had quadriplegia and been in that condition for thirty-eight years. He lay at the poolside because once a year an Angel came and stirred the water healing the diseases of whoever got in first:

> *Now there is at Jerusalem by the sheep market a pool, which is called in the Hebrew tongue Bethesda, having five porches. In these lay a great multitude of impotent folk, of blind, halt, withered, waiting for the moving of the water. For an angel went down at a certain season into the pool, and troubled the water: whosoever then first after the troubling of the water stepped in was made whole of whatsoever disease he had. And a certain man was there, which had an infirmity thirty and eight years. When Jesus saw him lie, and knew that he had been now a long time in that case, he saith unto him, Wilt thou be made whole? The impotent man answered him, Sir, I have no man, when the water is troubled, to put me into*

the pool: but while I am coming, another steppeth down before me. Jesus saith unto him,
Rise, take up thy bed, and walk. And immediately the man was made whole, and took up
his bed, and walked: and on the same day was the sabbath (John 5:2-9).

The scriptures take the time to inform the reader that the building he was in had
FIVE porches. Do you remember the symbology of the number 5? The five porches are
supposed to tell us that this is a place of Grace and Mercy. What about the number 38?
It has no meaning on its own except we remember that the Trials of the Elect are to be
cut short by Christ; otherwise, the coming destruction would destroy all flesh. 40 is the
number of Trials and Tribulation. The man's trial was cut short:

> *For then shall be great tribulation, such as was not since the beginning of the world to this*
> *time, no, nor ever shall be. And except those days should be shortened, there should no flesh*
> *be saved: but for the elect's sake, those days shall be shortened* (Matt. 24:21-22).

Jesus came and saw the man in that condition with no one helping him. He healed
the man and asked him to go home. The esoteric meaning of the story is that you could
be in a church building, a mosque, a synagogue, or a temple, looking for help and mercy,
but never receive it. However, if you are there and call on the name of Jesus, he will come
and save you. Just be sure to take your bed and GO HOME after that.

The final miracle we will investigate was not so much supernatural transformation
of a physical substance or person, but the transformation of a group of people by his
prophetic gift. This miracle is the story regarding the Woman at the well. As the story
goes, Jesus was waiting for his disciples by a well of water. A woman who was Samaritan
came to draw water from the well (Judaic considered Samaritans as untouchables). Jesus
asked her to give him water to drink. She was puzzled and asked him why he would ask
a Samaritan for water:

> *Jesus answered and said unto her, If thou knewest the gift of God, and who it is that saith*
> *to thee, Give me to drink; thou wouldest have asked of him, and he would have given thee*
> *living water* (Jn. 4:10).

The woman asked him for the living water, but he tested her by asking her to go call
her husband. She responded earnestly by saying she had no husband. Jesus surprised her
by telling her that she had had five husbands and that even the man she was living with
now was not her husband:

The woman saith unto him, Sir, give me this water, that I thirst not, neither come hither to draw. Jesus saith unto her, Go, call thy husband, and come hither. The woman answered and said, I have no husband. Jesus said unto her, Thou hast well said, I have no husband<u>: For thou hast had five husbands; and he whom thou now hast is not thy husband: in that saidst thou truly</u>. The woman saith unto him, Sir, I perceive that thou art a prophet. Our fathers worshipped in this mountain; and ye say, that in Jerusalem is the place where men ought to worship. Jesus saith unto her, Woman, believe me, the hour cometh, when ye shall neither in this mountain, nor yet at Jerusalem, worship the Father (Jn. 4:15-21).

She was shocked and ran to call the people in town, saying that she might have met the Prophet to come. The people came and believed. If she had five husbands in the past, and the man she was with now was not her husband, what number would Jesus have been in her life? The 7th man. Look up the symbolic meaning of the number 7 in our previous table. We all need to have a relationship with the 7th Man.

Four books tell us about the life of Jesus. These are Matthew, Mark, Luke, and John. The *Synoptic* Gospels are how we refer to the first three books because they have a similarity in content and chronology of events. The book of John, on the other hand, has a different perspective in the way it both understands Jesus and the activities it catalogs concerning his ministry. While the first three books describe his humanity, the book of John begins with his divinity.

In the book of John, it opens with this account about Jesus. *"In the beginning was the Word. The Word was with God, and the Word was God"* (Jn.1:1). This beginning is not a chronological beginning, as in some period in the history of the Universe. It refers to a spiritual essence that precedes the initiation of any activity related to man. So, for example, tomorrow, you might be urged by God to do something. The "beginning" of that thing ought to be initiated by the Word of God. The Greek used here for "Word" is "Logos," which has a whole deeper meaning than just "Word" or "Reason." It is beyond the scope of this book to elaborate on that. However, we might be able to in future writings. So, understanding the esoteric meaning of the Gospels and what they indicate is a prerequisite for being able to interpret the messages contained in his parables, teachings, events, and miracles.

Central to Jesus' teaching is the concept of the Kingdom of God being imminent. When asked when and where the Kingdom was, he responded that it was within us. His teaching centered around the fact that all human beings are born dead, and they needed to be "Born Again" to be able to comprehend the direction into the Kingdom. So, his message was not complicated. Being born again means experiencing a rebirth of the spirit, and considering the teachings of the prophets far inferior to his doctrine, unable to deliver an adherent into the Kingdom of God.

> *Then said Jesus unto them again, Verily, verily, I say unto you, I am the door of the sheep. All that ever came before me are thieves and robbers: but the sheep did not hear them. I am the door: by me if any man enter in, he shall be saved, and shall go in and out, and find pasture* (Jn. 10:7-9).

Every action he took during his three and a half years of ministry was symbolic of some more in-depth esoteric teaching. Whether it was walking on water, rubbing sand on the eyes of the blind, the transfiguration, healing lepers, etc. All these acts have esoteric meanings directly relevant to you and I. For example, the healing of lepers signifies the transformation of your soul from being **INSENSITIVE** to the heart of God. Rubbing sand in the eyes to heal the blind signifies his use of seemingly insignificant events in our lives to teach us and enlighten our understanding. Walking on water indicates our ability to bypass the law of nature if need be to do his will. The transfiguration was symbolic of the new bodies we will receive in the Resurrection:

> *Behold, I shew you a mystery; We shall not all sleep, but we shall all be changed, In a moment, in the twinkling of an eye, at the last trump: for the trumpet shall sound, and the dead shall be raised incorruptible, <u>and we shall be changed</u>. For this corruptible must put on incorruption, and this mortal must put on immortality* (1 Cor. 15:51-53).

It is important to understand one crucial factor regarding the doctrine of Jesus. His commandments to us were not intended to be accomplished in our strength, or by our efforts. The subtle work of the Holy Ghost fulfills these commandments in, and through us. This is the power that was to come after his Resurrection. So, if we read the bible and see where Jesus says *"be ye therefore perfect as your father in heaven is perfect"* (Matt. 5:48), or *"Love your enemies, and do good to those who hate you"* (Lk. 6:27), these are not virtues that are naturally inherent in us by birth. Even when we practice them as "good" people outside of the grace and power of the Holy Ghost, it counts for nothing in his sight. The only thing that counts for something is that which is accomplished **BY** the Holy Ghost **THROUGH** us. Therefore, because of the transformative work of regeneration by the Holy Ghost, a person with a changed nature, will effortlessly love her enemies, and do good to those who hate her without even realizing this is what she does consistently.

Another aspect of Jesus' doctrine which people misunderstand, just as his disciples did, was the Oneness of the Saints in heaven and earth. A Saint is anyone who puts his trust in God through Jesus Christ. Now, saints include those of the Old Testament, who would later come to believe AFTER his resurrection. (Matt. 27:51-53). The event known as the Transfiguration is an example of this doctrine of Oneness. Specifically, Jesus' statement about Abraham, Isaac, and Jacob to the Judaics.

We will elaborate on this a little here. In Luke Chapter 20, Jesus explains to the Sadducees and scribes that those who have died are not dead. That even now, they are interacting with God and us, although we cannot see them. He uses the example of God, introducing himself to Moses by saying he is the God of Abraham, Isaac, and Jacob. What astonished the hearers was Jesus' interpretation of that account. He was connoting that the three patriarchs were still alive while Moses was speaking with God:

> *But they which shall be accounted worthy to obtain that world, and the resurrection from the dead, neither marry, nor are given in marriage: Neither can they die any more: for they are equal unto the angels; and are the children of God, being the children of the resurrection. Now that the dead are raised, even Moses shewed at the bush, when he calleth the Lord the God of Abraham, and the God of Isaac, and the God of Jacob. For he is not a God of the dead, but of the living: for all live unto him* (Lk.20:35-38).

Even the Apostle Paul would later pick up on this doctrine in Hebrews 12 to say that we are currently surrounded by a *great cloud of witnesses* that included all the bible heroes that had preceded us:

> *Wherefore seeing <u>we also are compassed about with so great a cloud of witnesses,</u> let us lay aside every weight, and the sin which doth so easily beset us, and let us run with patience the race that is set before us, Looking unto Jesus the author and finisher of our faith; who for the joy that was set before him endured the cross, despising the shame, and is set down at the right hand of the throne of God* (Heb. 12:1-2).

The people and Jesus' disciples abandoned him to the Judaic rulers despite everything he had done for them. Nevertheless, all this was part of the plan of God. Next, we will look at the victory in his death.

JESUS' DEATH AND RESURRECTION

RIGHT FROM THE GARDEN OF EDEN, GOD MADE A PROMISE THAT a "seed" would be born who would "break the head" of the serpent:

And the LORD God said unto the serpent, Because thou hast done this, thou art cursed above all cattle, and above every beast of the field; upon thy belly shalt thou go, and dust shalt thou eat all the days of thy life: And I will put enmity between thee and the woman, and between thy seed and her seed; it shall bruise thy head, <u>and thou shalt bruise his heel</u> (Gen. 3:14-15).

The serpent was symbolic of Satanic power.

Now the death of Jesus occurred in this manner. He had twelve Apostles and many other disciples. They all were hoping that Jesus would take power from the Romans and Herod (Herod was an Edomite) and establish a Kingdom on earth, with them as viceroys (Luke 24:13-35). However, only one, Judas, tried to force the issue, because his greed was overwhelming for him. He did not intend for Jesus to die. He believed Jesus was the Messiah. Every Judaic who believed in Messiah thought that as the Son of God, he could not die because the prophecies stated that his Kingdom would be forever. Therefore, when Judas saw that Jesus had died, he hung himself, saying he had killed "an innocent man," not the Messiah:

When the morning was come, all the chief priests and elders of the people took counsel against Jesus to put him to death: And when they had bound him, they led him away, and delivered him to Pontius Pilate the governor. Then Judas, which had betrayed him, <u>when he saw that he was condemned,</u> repented himself, and brought again the thirty pieces of silver to the chief priests and elders, Saying, I have sinned in that I have betrayed the *innocent blood. And they said, What is that to us? see thou to that. And he cast down the pieces of silver in the temple, and departed, and went and hanged himself* (Matt 27:1-5}.

The Passover Feast occurs around the 17th Day of the Month of Abib (Around April). The night BEFORE Judas betrayed him; he took his disciples to a house where he ministered an oath to them. He symbolically ate bread and drank wine with them as a sign of a covenant relationship with him. This ritual was something none of them should have done if they had no intention of keeping the oath. Immediately Judas ate the bread; Satan entered him (Jn. 13:27). It is crucial to point out that Jesus died BEFORE the Hebrew Feast of Passover. Therefore, his death was NOT per the Levitical requirements, but after the obligations of a different Priestly Order, the Order of Melchizedek. The Levitical Order required a sacrifice of the Lamb on THE DAY of Passover. They sacrificed Jesus BEFORE Passover.

Judas went to the Rabbis and Priests with an offer to show them where Jesus was, so they could capture him. He felt that Jesus would have no choice but to prove to them that he was the Messiah. He received from them THIRTY pieces of Silver. If you remember our chapter on the numeric significance of numbers, you will recall that Thirty is the number for Maturity, and Silver is representative of Redemption. So, Judas had unwittingly sold his Salvation for thirty pieces of Silver. This was in fulfillment of scripture in Zechariah about thirty pieces of silver, and a potter's field (Matt. 26:15).

The prophecy in Zechariah says:

I told them, "If you think it best, give me my pay; but if not, keep it." So, they paid me thirty pieces of silver. And the Lord said to me, "Throw it to the potter"—the handsome price at which they valued me! So, I took the thirty pieces of silver and threw them to the potter at the house of the Lord (Zech. 11:12-13).

When they arrived, they came with soldiers. It is important to note that these soldiers were not Roman soldiers, but Soldiers of the Temple. A sort of Judaic militia permitted to guard the Temple since Gentiles were not allowed in there. The High Priests asked Jesus if he claimed to be the Son of God. They kept beating him to either renounce his position or say something against Caesar. He kept quiet.

Finally, they sent him to Pontius Pilate, the Roman Governor of Judaea, for the death sentence since the Judaic authority did not have the power of the death sentence. When they brought him before Pilate, he kept quiet while the interrogation lasted. He spoke very little, and Pilate decided to set him free because he could find nothing that Jesus had done against Roman or Judaic law that required the death sentence. When the Judaic saw that he was about to set Jesus free, they accused Jesus of making himself a King in place of Caesar. They threatened Pilate by saying anyone who would keep Jesus alive was no friend of Caesar.

For this reason, Pilate acquiesced and gave Jesus over to them to do with him as they pleased. They crucified him but were surprised that he died so quickly. They expected he and the other prisoners to die the next day, the Feast of Passover:

> *The Jews therefore, because it was the preparation, that the bodies should not remain upon the cross on the sabbath day, (for that sabbath day was an high day,) besought Pilate that their legs might be broken, and that they might be taken away. Then came the soldiers, and brake the legs of the first, and of the other which was crucified with him. But when they came to Jesus, and saw that he was dead already, they brake not his legs: But one of the soldiers with a spear pierced his side, and forthwith came there out blood and water* (Jn. 19:31-34).

Jesus died sooner than they expected to fulfill his statement that said:

> *Therefore doth my Father love me, because I lay down my life, that I might take it again. No man taketh it from me, but I lay it down of myself. I have power to lay it down, and I have power to take it again. This commandment have I received of my Father* (Jn. 10:17-18).

They buried him in the tomb of one of his secret disciples called Joseph of Arimathea, a rich man. On the third day, he rose from the dead and appeared to many of his followers. He ate with them and told them to wait for the coming of the Holy Ghost. The Spirit would bring us a deeper understanding of what Jesus had been teaching.

As mentioned earlier, every account in the Old Testament is directly or indirectly analogous to the Life, Death, and Resurrection of Christ. You also recall that we said Christ is the combination of Jesus and his Body, the Elect. So, Jesus Christ was the first from the dead, just as a head is what comes forth first from the mother at birth:

> *And, behold, the veil of the temple was rent in twain from the top to the bottom; and the earth did quake, and the rocks rent; <u>And the graves were opened; and many bodies of the saints which slept arose, And came out of the graves after his resurrection,</u> and went into the holy city, and appeared unto many. Now when the centurion, and they that were with him,*

watching Jesus, saw the earthquake, and those things that were done, they feared greatly, saying, Truly this was the Son of God (Matt. 27:51-54).

The crucifixion of Christ was the fulfillment of the bruising of the heel. The opening of the graves and the dead arising was the breaking of the serpents head.

You recall that Moses and the children of Israel had to sacrifice a lamb and dab the lintels of their doors with the blood of the lamb to protect them from the Angel of Death that was to kill all First-born males. John the Baptist understood the esoteric meaning of that event. *"The next day John seeth Jesus coming unto him, and saith, Behold the Lamb of God, which taketh away the sin of the world. when he proclaimed"* (Jn. 1:29). The blood of Moses' Lambs COVERED the people, but the blood of Jesus CLEANSED away our sins.

The prophet Isaiah prophesied about his death and resurrection in chapter 53 of the book of Isaiah that *"Surely he has borne our griefs and carried our sorrows....... He was wounded for our transgressions and bruised for our iniquities"* (Is. 53:1-12). The prophet Hosea also foresaw the suffering of death by Jesus and the glory that would be revealed after. He said:

> *Come and let us return unto the LORD: for he hath torn, and he will heal us; he hath smitten, and he will bind us up. After two days will he revive us: in the third day he will raise us up, and we shall live in his sight. Then shall we know, if we follow on to know the LORD: his going forth is prepared as the morning; and he shall come unto us as the rain, as the latter and former rain unto the earth* (Hos. 6:1-3).

Here we can see the prophet forecasting the THIRD DAY resurrection, which we now know has occurred. We, however, await the FOURTH DAY resurrection.

The primary purpose of the death of the "Only-begotten Son of God" was to act as a planted seed to multiply the number of sons available to God. *"Verily, verily, I say unto you, Except a corn of wheat fall into the ground and die, it abideth alone: but if it die, it bringeth forth much fruit "*(Jn. 12:24). His sufferings during his life, as well as during his crucifixion, was a necessary ritual intended as a means for him to partake in the miseries that we currently experience so that he might be able to share our burdens. For this reason, no matter what trials we face, we have a comforter that is more than able to lift any weights of our shoulders:

> *But we see Jesus, who was made a little lower than the angels for the suffering of death, crowned with glory and honour; that he by the grace of God should taste death for every*

man. For it became him, for whom are all things, and by whom are all things, in bringing many sons unto glory, to make the captain of their salvation perfect through sufferings. For both he that sanctifieth and they who are sanctified are all of one: for which cause he is not ashamed to call them brethren (Heb. 2:9-11).

Notice that the intent was to "bring many sons into glory."

We need to point out some moral lessons concerning the Resurrection of Jesus. First, he did not appear to his male disciples, until after he appeared to the women first. He instructed them to go tell the Apostles that he has risen. The moral of this story is to show that Jesus gave the gospel to women first. Therefore, anyone stopping women from preaching is opposing Jesus. When the Apostle Paul is translated as saying women should not "teach," he is being mistranslated. He even named a woman, Junia, as an Apostle before him in Christ. The Greek word translated as "Teach" that Paul used in the book of Timothy is "Didache," which means to DICTATE. *"Let the woman learn in silence with all subjection. But I suffer not a woman to teach, nor to usurp authority over the man, but to be in silence"* (1 Tim. 2:11-12) He did not want women dictating over men. They can teach, but not be in a position of authority over men in the church.

Secondly, Jesus gave instructions for the believers in Jerusalem not to go into ministry until the Holy Ghost had come upon them:

> *To whom also he shewed himself alive after his passion by many infallible proofs, being seen of them forty days, and speaking of the things pertaining to the kingdom of God: Wait for the Holy Spirit And, being assembled together with them, commanded them that they should not depart from Jerusalem, but wait for the promise of the Father, which, saith he, ye have heard of me. For John truly baptized with water; but ye shall be baptized with the Holy Ghost not many days hence* (Acts. 1:3-5).

There were five hundred disciples to whom he gave this instruction. However, on the day the Holy Ghost came, only one hundred and twenty were in the place of prayer.

Thirdly, during the forty days, he was on earth after his resurrection, he would appear from time to time unexpectedly and eat with them. What is significant about this is that after his resurrection, he could walk through walls and yet, had no blood in his body:

> *And he said unto them, Why are ye troubled? and why do thoughts arise in your hearts? Behold my hands and my feet, that it is I myself: handle me, and see; for a spirit hath*

not flesh and bones, as ye see me have. And when he had thus spoken, he shewed them his hands and his feet. And while they yet believed not for joy, and wondered, he said unto them, Have ye here any meat? And they gave him a piece of a broiled fish, and of an honeycomb. And he took it, and did eat before them (Lk. 24:38-43).

This discussion begins to give us an indication of what the spiritual body of the resurrected saints will resemble. We will be on earth with a body that can do the same things.

Finally, his biggest concern before he left was that those who were more mature should look after his sheep. "*He saith unto him the third time, Simon, son of Jonas, lovest thou me? Peter was grieved because he said unto him the third time, Lovest thou me? And he said unto him, Lord, thou knowest all things; thou knowest that I love thee. Jesus saith unto him, Feed my sheep*" (Jn. 21:17). We who are called higher must never underappreciate the seriousness of this request from Christ. **I ask him to forgive me for all that I have done foolishly to demoralize his sheep.**

THE DOCTRINE OF
THE HOLY GHOST

I N SUMMARY, EVERYTHING THAT OCCURRED IN THE OLD TESTAMENT
and within the Gospels was a kind of foreshadowing of the experiences that we as
individuals would have in the ages following the ascension of Jesus Christ. This
foreshadowing means that we can find nuggets of direction within the minor and major
details in Old Testament accounts, as well as the Gospels.

There were three principal Feasts that God commanded the Israelites to keep as well
as a few minor feasts. The three principal feasts were first Passover, then the second was
Pentecost, and the third was the Feast of Tabernacles. According to the New Testament,
Jesus fulfilled the spiritual Passover feast by his death, and the spiritual Feast of Pentecost
by the outpouring of the Holy Spirit. The feast yet to be fulfilled by Jesus is the Feast of
Tabernacles. The feast of Tabernacles is the fulfillment of the search for the Kingdom.
The final descent of God into mankind in all fullness possible:

> *And I John saw the holy city, new Jerusalem, coming down from God out of heaven,*
> *prepared as a bride adorned for her husband. And I heard a great voice out of heaven*
> *saying, Behold, the tabernacle of God is with men, and he will dwell with them, and they*
> *shall be his people, and God himself shall be with them, and be their God* (Rev. 21:2-3).

According to Mosaic law, fifty days after Passover is the Feast of Pentecost. The
book of Acts indicates when the Feast of Pentecost had fully come, a sound like a mighty
wind came to where the Apostles and Disciples were praying. The Holy Ghost and
Power filled one hundred and twenty of them. They also began to speak in tongues.
On that day, three thousand people who heard them became believers in Christ and
accepted the truth about Jesus. It was contrary to the day that Moses brought the Ten
Commandments, and three thousand people died. Jesus ascended to Heaven in front of

his disciples, in a "Cloud." We should remember this word, Cloud because we are going to confront it several times in the scriptures. It refers to the "Crowd" of heavenly people, not a natural cloud. *"And when he had spoken these things, while they beheld, he was taken up; and a cloud received him out of their sight "*(Acts. 1:9). Also, in the book of Hebrews, he tells us that some heavenly people have their eyes on us right now. *"Wherefore seeing we also are compassed about with so great a cloud of witnesses, let us lay aside every weight, and the sin which doth so easily beset us, and let us run with patience the race that is set before us "*(Heb. 12:1).

The third feast, Tabernacles, is the essence of everything we are hoping for in this faith. It is the desire of the ages. Many scriptures that refer to the last trumpet, the coming of Christ, the wedding feast, etc. are all different ways of articulating the significance of this feast to the eventual goal of the believer. This feast of tabernacles, as mentioned earlier, is symbolic of the time when God himself will come down to dwell In and with man in all his fullness:

> *For as in Adam all die, even so in Christ shall all be made alive. But every man in his own order: Christ the firstfruits; afterward they that are Christ's at his coming. Then cometh the end, when he shall have delivered up the kingdom to God, even the Father; when he shall have put down all rule and all authority and power. For he must reign, till he hath put all enemies under his feet. The last enemy that shall be destroyed is death. For he hath put all things under his feet. But when he saith, all things are put under him, it is manifest that he is excepted, which did put all things under him. And when all things shall be subdued unto him, then shall the Son also himself be subject unto him that put all things under him, that God may be all in all* (1 Cor. 15:22-28).

These verses are speaking about the Feast of Tabernacles but in an esoteric form. Notice that it says in the last verse, that "God may be all in all." Earlier it states that in the end, "the Son" shall also be subject to the Father. What could this mean? Is Jesus Christ not subject to the Father? Has he not demonstrated that, even to the point of death? Well, the Son he is referring to here is not Jesus, but those given the "call to Sonship." Those who can read this and understand. It is they who must bring "Death" under control so that "God may be all in All."

After the Holy Ghost came down on the Feast of Pentecost, the Christians began to win many converts because of the miracles that the Holy Ghost was doing through them. This conversion displeased the Judaic leaders who had persecuted Jesus. They imprisoned and beat many of the disciples, but this only helped spread the Word of God. They even went as far as killing James, an Apostle, not the brother of Jesus, and

Stephen, a Deacon. Among the people who persecuted the Christians was a young zealous Pharisee named Saul of Tarsus. Later to become Paul the Apostle.

Now, if we remember at the beginning of this book, we had mentioned how God commanded mankind to be fruitful and replenish the earth after Noah. However, people decided to stick together in one place and build a tower and a city. Well, the same thing began to happen with the church. They all remained in Jerusalem, instead of preaching the gospel worldwide, as instructed by Jesus. So, God allowed great persecution to come upon the church, causing them to flee out of Jerusalem. This persecution made them take the gospel all over the world:

"As for Saul, he made havock of the church, entering into every house, and haling men and women committed them to prison. Therefore, they that were scattered abroad went everywhere preaching the word" (Acts 8:3-4). *"Now they which were scattered abroad upon the persecution that arose about Stephen travelled as far as Phenice, and Cyprus, and Antioch, preaching the word to none but unto the Jews only"* (Acts. 11:19-20).

Now we can see from the scripture in Acts Chapter 8 from verse 3 to 4 that even before Paul became a Christian, Christ was using him to spread the gospel. How? His persecution of the church scattered the Christians, and they began to preach outside of Jerusalem, and even Judea.

The Holy Ghost is the third emanation of the Triune God. This emanation sometimes confuses people, so that they distinguish him from God or Jesus Christ. The best way to understand the Holy Ghost is to know him as Jesus Christ manifested in his Glory, and the Father manifested comprehensibly. So, we have, on the one hand, God, and on the other hand, we have Jesus Christ the Man. In Jesus Christ, we have the Father, the Son, and the Holy Ghost. In God, we also have the Father, the Son, and the Holy Spirit. The difference is that in his fullness as God, he is incomprehensible and can never be seen or understood:

"Believe me that I am in the Father, and the Father in me: or else believe me for the very works' sake "(Jn. 14:11).

"That thou keep this commandment without spot, unrebukeable, until the appearing of our Lord Jesus Christ: Which in his times he shall shew, who is the blessed and only Potentate, the King of kings, and Lord of lords; Who only hath immortality, <u>dwelling in the light which no man can approach unto; whom no man hath seen,</u> nor can see: to whom be honour and power everlasting. Amen. "(1 Tim. 6:14-16).

The agency by which we can both comprehend God and Jesus Christ is the Holy Spirit. Without him, we cannot understand God or Jesus Christ. Without this understanding, we cannot have Eternal Life. *"And this is life eternal, that they might know thee the only true God, and Jesus Christ, whom thou hast sent. "*(Jn. 17:3).

The manifest presence of God that experiences the pain, suffering, and temptation of mankind is Jesus Christ. The manifest presence of God that gives mankind the power to overcome these things, just as Jesus did, is the Holy Spirit. This one-person, God, is the Father, the Son, and the Holy Spirit. It is the Holy Ghost that guided the Apostles and the Christians in the early days of the church and continues to do so today. He determines where and when to plant churches, to travel, and who should lead the assembly.

The doctrine of the Holy Ghost intends to bring people to a full assurance of salvation through belief in Jesus Christ. Any person being used by him would often seek to give glory to God through Jesus Christ. One of the most important teachings of the Holy Ghost is that in which he wants people to know that they are no longer under the Law but under the benefit of his Grace.

The early church was made up primarily of the Jews, who had believed in Jesus. Nevertheless, they still held firmly to the Laws of Moses and opposed the Apostle Paul everywhere he went and planted a church. They would go behind him to tell the people that they must be circumcised according to the Law of Moses; otherwise, they could not be saved. This teaching was not the doctrine of the Holy Ghost. When the controversy became too much, they agreed with Paul to head to Jerusalem to meet with the elders of the church, primarily Peter, James, and John. The elders ruled in Paul's favor, but that did not stop the Jewish Christians from continuing to go after Paul:

> *And certain men which came down from Judaea taught the brethren, and said, Except ye be circumcised after the manner of Moses, ye cannot be saved. When therefore Paul and Barnabas had no small dissension and disputation with them, they determined that Paul and Barnabas, and certain other of them, should go up to Jerusalem unto the apostles and elders about this question* (Acts 15:1-2).

This account is very important, as the struggle that began then continues to this day, within the church: namely Old Testament doctrines adopted by Christians, which contradict the teachings of the Holy Ghost.

As we read in our analysis of the Old Testament, sin dominated all men, even the Righteous men of God like Adam, Abraham, Moses, David, etc. The consequence of this was that God could not fully inhabit man as his intent was:

> *And David my servant shall be king over them; and they all shall have one shepherd: they shall also walk in my judgments, and observe my statutes, and do them. And they shall dwell in the land that I have given unto Jacob my servant, wherein your fathers have dwelt; and they shall dwell therein, even they, and their children, and their children's children for ever: and my servant David shall be their prince for ever. Moreover I will make a covenant of peace with them; it shall be an everlasting covenant with them: and I will place them, and multiply them, <u>and will set my sanctuary in the midst of them for evermore</u>. My tabernacle also shall be with them: yea, I will be their God, and they shall be my people* (Ez. 37:24-27).

His very presence would have been eternally destructive to us. Therefore, internal cleansing must first take place, and then a raising of the consciousness to an appreciation of that state. Jesus accomplished the first. The Holy Spirit is currently conducting the latter.

The consciousness of sin serves as a barrier to the relationship between man and God. Even when God forgives a man for sins, his conscience can still deceive him into believing that he is still unrighteous in the presence of God. The purpose of the Holy Ghost is to persuade those who have believed in Jesus that God has forgiven them and that there is no condemnation awaiting them. The purpose of this is primarily twofold; first to bring peace into the hearts of mankind, and second to give God what he has always craved; a relationship with someone who can relate with him based on her autonomous conviction. *"And they heard the voice of the LORD God walking in the garden in the cool of the day: and Adam and his wife hid themselves from the presence of the LORD God amongst the trees of the garden. "*(Gen. 3:8).

Now each person has some degree of confidence in what she feels is permissible by her God and what she feels is impermissible. Cultural outlook and personal experience influence this certainty, but the Holy Ghost can unveil the distinctions over time. Two believers don't have to argue over things that are not explicitly commanded or rejected in New Testament scripture concerning mankind. Secondly, it is vital to make a distinction between the Levitical Laws and the Moral Laws. Moral Laws are belief systems that are often universal — laws like those against stealing, or Murder. However, Laws like paying of Tithes, worshiping on specified days, monogamy versus polygamy, dress patterns, etc. are left to the individual and her God.

There is one Law that puts all these Laws in harmony. The Commandment to Love our neighbor as ourselves. According to the doctrine of the Holy Ghost, because I have the Right to conduct myself in a way that my neighbor feels objectionable, it doesn't mean that God is pleased with me when I exercise this Right. I should be considerate to the deeply held conscience of others as I practice my Rights, and exercise my liberties:

> *I know, and am persuaded by the Lord Jesus, that there is nothing unclean of itself: but to him that esteemeth any thing to be unclean, to him it is unclean. But if thy brother be grieved with thy meat, now walkest thou not charitably. Destroy not him with thy meat, for whom Christ died. Let not then your good be evil spoken of: For the kingdom of God is not meat and drink; but righteousness, and peace, and joy in the Holy Ghost. For he that in these things serveth Christ is acceptable to God, and approved of men. Let us therefore follow after the things which make for peace, and things wherewith one may edify another. For meat destroy not the work of God. All things indeed are pure; but it is evil for that man who eateth with offence. It is good neither to eat flesh, nor to drink wine, nor any thing whereby thy brother stumbleth, or is offended, or is made weak. Hast thou faith? have it to thyself before God. Happy is he that condemneth not himself in that thing which he alloweth. And he that doubteth is damned if he eat, because he eateth not of faith: for whatsoever is not of faith is sin." (Rom. 14:13-23). "We then that are strong ought to bear the infirmities of the weak, and not to please ourselves. Let every one of us please his neighbour for his good to edification"* (Rom. 15:1).

This consideration is the sign of maturity for a follower of Christ.

On the other hand, there are believers who, by their stubborn attachment to what they consider to be holy practices, unwittingly lockout from the Kingdom, those outsiders who are unlearned in the way of Christ, and who we must welcome in as they are. For example, some want to know Christ but have grown up in other religions where they learned to pray five times a day, facing one direction or another, or have grown up praying through what they consider to be saints or ancestors. Some of these persons might be able to immediately drop those forms of worship once they hear the truth of Christ, but others might need more time to assimilate the meaning of what they have learned. Love demands that we walk appropriately as God has shown us so that when they mature to know better, they can remember us for an example. We should teach the truth in Love but let them be. *"But speaking the truth in love, may grow up into him in all things, which is the head, even Christ "*(Eph. 4:15).

In geology, abrasion is the shaping of huge rocks over time by the wind. This abrasion is the kind of work the Holy Ghost does in the lives of individuals who have come to believe in Christ. He can take a long patient time working from the inside out and shaping an individual to become like Christ. Not to become like you or I. Understanding the Holy Ghost and his ways gives an individual a massive advantage over others in this way.

The nature of Sin is a topic that God had sought to explain to Cain while he contemplated killing his brother:

> *And the LORD said unto Cain, Why art thou wroth? and why is thy countenance fallen? If thou doest well, shalt thou not be accepted? and if thou doest not well, sin lieth at the door. And unto thee shall be his desire, and thou shalt rule over him"* *(Gen. 4:6-7).*

In trying to explain this, I will digress a little into science as an example.

Sin is like the Force of Gravity in the physical sciences. Gravity is the pull of a Mass or Object on another Mass or Object. For example, the natural Sun has a Mass that is enormous compared to the Mass of the Earth. The earth, in turn, has a Mass that is greater than the size of Mass that composes your natural body. So, Gravity created by the Sun's mass pulls the earth while gravity created by the earth's Mass pulls your body. That pull of the earth on your Mass is what we call "Weight." So, Allegorically the weight of sins is on us because we have not had it washed away by the blood of Christ. Hence the sense of guilt:

> *Wherefore seeing we also are compassed about with so great a cloud of witnesses, let us lay aside every weight, and the sin which doth so easily beset us, and let us run with patience the race that is set before us* (Heb. 12:1).

The further a Mass is from the Sun, multiplied by the size of that Mass your body weight on it might feel lighter or heavier. So, if you were to go to the moon, you would find that you have "lost weight." However, you're technically the same amount of mass, but because the moon is smaller in Mass than the earth, even though they are relatively similar in distance from the sun. Of course, because the Moon revolves around the earth as it circles the sun, the moon is sometimes closer to the sun than the earth is, and at other times it is further from the sun than the earth is.

Your question would be, "okay, I get it about the Forces of Gravity, etc. but what does this have to do with Sin?" Well, remember how we said that Elisha helped the young prophets who had lost their Axe head in the river by throwing in a dry stick, which caused the Axe head to float? Well, the ax-head represents Sin, while the dry stick represents Jesus Christ:

> *And the sons of the prophets said unto Elisha, Behold now, the place where we dwell with thee is too strait for us. Let us go, we pray thee, unto Jordan, and take thence every man a beam, and let us make us a place there, where we may dwell. And he answered, Go ye. And one said, Be content, I pray thee, and go with thy servants. And he answered, I will go. So he went with them. And when they came to Jordan, they cut down wood. But as one was felling a beam, the axe head fell into the water: and he cried, and said, Alas, master! for it was borrowed. And the man of God said, Where fell it? And he shewed him the place. And he cut down a stick, and cast it in thither; and the iron did swim Therefore said he, Take it up to thee. And he put out his hand, and took it"* (2 Kg. 6 1-6).

He became Sin for us so that we could become the righteousness of God.

Each of us has the effect of some gravitational pull of sin. Depending on our relative distance from a peculiar sin, we might not be too affected by it. Sometimes, because of social and family circumstances beyond our control, we might find that from a young age, we have certain negative traits that are abhorrent to God and ourselves. However, try as we may, we are unable to resist the temptation to engage in that sin. This temptation is where the power of Christ comes in." *For he hath made him to be sin for us, who knew no sin; that we might be made the righteousness of God in him"* (2 Cor. 5:21). Given time, he will deliver you and me from the power of any sin.

Over time, because you have come to an understanding of who he is, you find that the force of influence from the debilitating sin begins to recede, and your ability to do what is pleasing to God becomes stronger. So, if we see a person struggling with what we consider to be a big sin relative to ours, we must remember that depending on her proximity to that condition at some earlier point in time, she must deal with a greater pull from that sin than we do. Nevertheless, she should be unhappy in that situation, and not openly celebrating her weakness. *Her dissatisfaction with the situation is her evidence that she is a child of God.*

Wherefore, my brethren, ye also are become dead to the law by the body of Christ; that ye should be married to another, even to him who is raised from the dead, that we should bring forth fruit unto God (Rom. 7:24).

We must understand the Old Testament for what it is. An account of God's dealings with certain peoples at a point in time, as a means of conveying a spiritual message to all mankind. The Levitical Laws, though sometimes helpful, are not required to be observed by the believer in Christ. Often people bring up the statement of Jesus in which he said:

Do not think that I have come to abolish the Law or the Prophets; I have not come to abolish them but to fulfill them. For truly I tell you, until heaven and earth disappear, not the smallest letter, not the least stroke of a pen, will by any means disappear from the Law until everything is accomplished. <u>Therefore, anyone who sets aside one of the least of these commands and teaches others accordingly will be called least in the kingdom of heaven, but whoever practices and teaches these commands will be called great in the kingdom of heaven.</u> For I tell you that unless your righteousness surpasses that of the Pharisees and the teachers of the law, you will certainly not enter the kingdom of heaven (Matt. 5:17-20).

If you remember, we said that Jesus was the last of the Old Testament prophets. His death and resurrection initiated the New Covenant, what we call the New Testament. His duty was to come and fulfill all the requirements of God under the Old Covenant, without making a mistake or sinning. This ability to resist sin he accomplished, and now fulfills through us by his Holy Spirit. God sees you now as perfectly fulfilling the requirements of the Moral Laws, through the blood of Jesus washes your conscience clean, and transforms you through the Holy Spirit.

This aspect of the doctrine of the Holy Ghost must be studied prayerfully and carefully. Our inability to understand this will hinder our ability to enter all that God has for us. It is this attachment to the Law that the forces of darkness utilize to keep us bound in fear:

And you, being dead in your sins and the uncircumcision of your flesh, hath he quickened together with him, having forgiven you all trespasses; Blotting out the handwriting of ordinances that was against us, which was contrary to us, and took it out of the way, nailing it to his cross; And having spoiled principalities and powers, he made a shew of them openly, triumphing over them in it. Let no man therefore judge you in meat, or in drink, or in respect of an holyday, or of the new moon, or of the sabbath days: Which are a shadow of things to come; but the body is of Christ (Col. 2:13-17).

The Law was an interim program to reaffirm the nature of God. It was not meant to be something observed mechanically. Situations and circumstances would arise in which keeping the Law would seem heartless. So, Jesus acknowledged that the Law was good, but demonstrated that Mercy was better.

For if the inheritance be of the law, it is no more of promise: but God gave it to Abraham by promise. <u>Wherefore then serveth the law? It was added because of transgressions, till the seed should come to whom the promise was made;</u> and it was ordained by angels in the hand of a mediator. Now a mediator is not a mediator of one, but God is one. Is the law then against the promises of God? God forbid: for if there had been a law given which could have given life, verily righteousness should have been by the law. But the scripture hath concluded all under sin, that the promise by faith of Jesus Christ might be given to them that believe. But before faith came, we were kept under the law, shut up unto the faith which should afterwards be revealed. <u>Wherefore the law was our schoolmaster to bring us unto Christ, that we might be justified by faith. But after that faith is come, we are no longer under a schoolmaster</u> (Gal. 3:1-29).

These scriptures show us that the Law is like a schoolteacher, sent to guide us until Christ came. Now that Christ has come, we have a new teacher, the Holy Ghost, who teaches us by changing us. It is no longer a matter of Will, but a Desire from within. If it is not from an inner desire, it is of "Works" or Human effort. None of which is acceptable to God according to the doctrine of the Holy Ghost.

Jesus made statements to us when he was physically here to make us see how difficult and impossible it was to meet the requirements of God by trying to keep the Law. We must know that this was his intention when he spoke about us being "perfect as God." You only need the sincerity of a child to know that it is impossible on your own to be perfect. *"But Jesus beheld them, and said unto them, With men this is impossible; but with God all things are possible. "*(Matt. 19:26).

The important thing to remember is that you are a coworker with God in making you into a habitation fit for him. *"For we are labourers together with God: ye are God's husbandry, ye are God's building"* (1 Cor. 3:9). (Eph. 2:22). Each person is a different part of the building. Some parts of the building must be built very slowly, others can be erected quickly, but none of them can be called a house without the other. *"In whom ye also are builded together for an habitation of God through the Spirit. "*(Eph. 2:22).

The problems come when the different parts of the building have no idea how the finished building is supposed to look. If the components parts could see and understand the blueprint, they, of course, would be more patient with each other. This book attempts to paint a clear picture of how to build the house and to show how it should look once finished. *"And look that thou make them after their pattern, which was shewed thee in the mount"* (Ex. 25:40).

In the Old Testament, God raised individuals to be Kings or Judges over all the people; however, now he is no longer using that method. The idea of one person being the Head over a Church or a group of churches is a kind of rebellion against the Headship of Christ. Does this mean that no persons can lead an assembly or churches? It does not mean that. All that is required is a group of individuals, scripturally referred to as Elders, have a common oversight over each assembly. However, it is not a Law that it be so. Often, an individual minister might find himself alone in virgin territory to plant a work of Christ. In such a situation, he would be the only person making decisions on spiritual matters until competent men and women develop the ability to join in leadership. At no time, however, should a woman alone head an Assembly for any extended period.

"Let the woman learn in silence with all subjection. But I suffer not a woman to teach, nor to usurp authority over the man, but to be in silence. For Adam was first formed, then Eve. And Adam was not deceived, but the woman being deceived was in the transgression" (1 Tim. 2:12).

The Holy Ghost is very concerned about the reputation of the Assembly to outsiders. For this reason, he encourages believers to live an upright lifestyle so that no dishonor falls on the name and reputation of Christ among the unlearned and unbelieving. So, even though a follower of Christ might feel free to drink a sip of wine now and then, the Holy Ghost might urge you not to do so in public or might go as far as stopping you entirely from drinking wine for the rest of your life. The degree to which he places burdens is also dependent on your ability to handle the demands. In almost no instance does he neglect you because you chose to exercise your own free will in Christ. *"It is good neither to eat flesh, nor to drink wine, nor any thing whereby thy brother stumbleth, or is offended, or is made weak. Hast thou faith? have it to thyself before God"* (Rom. 14:21-22).

The Holy Ghost is not pleased with believers who think to please God by observing the Levitical Laws. Especially in things like Sabbath Days, Tithes, not eating of specified foods, and other Levitical requirements.

"Let no man therefore judge you in meat, or in drink, or in respect of an holyday, or of the new moon, or of the sabbath days: Which are a shadow of things to come; but the body is of Christ" (Col. 2:16-17). *"Wherefore if ye be dead with Christ from the rudiments of the world, why, as though living in the world, are ye subject to ordinances, (Touch not; taste not; handle not; Which all are to perish with the using;) after the commandments and doctrines of men?"* (Col. 2:20-21).

The significance of keeping these outdated ordinances is that it seems to reflect that the follower of Christ doesn't recognize the death and resurrection of Christ as fully satisfying God's requirements for salvation.

Often, we read in the New Testament where an Apostle is complaining about people "walking in the flesh," and we assume he is referring to sinful acts like fornication, jealousy, lying, etc. but unfortunately, he might not be. He might be referring to things we do that we thought were Religiously right but are not motivated by the love of God or man. For example, in the book of Romans, chapter 7, The Holy Ghost says:

> *Wherefore, my brethren, ye also are <u>become dead to the law by the body of Christ;</u> that ye should be married to another, even to him who is raised from the dead, that we should bring forth fruit unto God. <u>For when we were in the flesh, the motions of sins, which were by the law, did work in our members to bring forth fruit unto death.</u> But now we are delivered from the law, that being dead wherein we were held; that we should serve in newness of spirit, and not in the oldness of the letter* (Rom. 7:4-6).

We can see here that the Holy Ghost is equating walking in the Law to walking in the flesh. His point was not that the Law was evil. His point was by trying to keep some part of the Law; obligates us to keep all of it. The problem therein is that no one can keep all the Law of God. He says it is the Law that causes the knowledge of sin:

> *What shall we say then? Is the law sin? God forbid. Nay, **I** <u>had not known sin, but by the law: for I had not known lust, except the law had said, Thou shalt not covet.</u> but sin, taking occasion by the commandment, wrought in me all manner of concupiscence. <u>For without the law sin was dead.</u> For I was alive without the law once: but when the commandment came, sin revived, and I died. And the commandment, which was ordained to life, I found to be unto death. For sin, taking occasion by the commandment, deceived me, and by it slew me* (Rom. 7:7-11).

The first verse of the next chapter contains the clincher. In it the Holy Ghost says:

> *There is therefore now no condemnation to them which are in Christ Jesus, who walk not after the flesh, but after the Spirit. For the law of the Spirit of life in Christ Jesus hath made me free from the law of sin and death. For what the law could not do, in that it was weak through the flesh, God sending his own Son in the likeness of sinful flesh, and for sin, condemned sin in the flesh: That the righteousness of the law might be fulfilled in us, who walk not after the flesh, but after the Spirit. For they that are after the flesh do mind the things of the flesh; but they that are after the Spirit the things of the Spirit. For to be carnally minded is death; but to be spiritually minded is life and peace. Because the carnal mind is enmity against God: for it is not subject to the law of God, neither indeed can be. So, then they that are in the flesh cannot please God* (Rom. 8:1-8).

The flesh it is referring to here is the human effort of following God according to our mental capacities in observance of the Laws of carnal commandments. In the past, we interpreted this scripture to refer to those who lived an unholy life. This interpretation is not the message in this teaching. The message is that if you are caught up in the ceremonials of your denomination, the carnal religious practices of your religion, and the face-value interpretation of the Old Testament Laws, you will be unable to comprehend the deeper teachings of God through the Holy Ghost. It is these teachings that have transformative capacity, not the surface level interpretation of scripture. So, to be "carnally minded" refers in the above context, to living religiously and in observance of the Law.

> *If therefore perfection were by the Levitical priesthood, (for under it the people received the law), what further need was there that another priest should rise after the order of Melchisedec, and not be called after the order of Aaron? For the priesthood being changed, there is made of necessity a change also of the law. For he of whom these things are spoken pertaineth to another tribe, of which no man gave attendance at the altar. For it is evident that our Lord sprang out of Judah; of which tribe Moses spake nothing concerning priesthood. And it is yet far more evident: for that after the similitude of Melchizedec there ariseth another priest, Who is made, not after the law of a carnal commandment, but after the power of an endless life* (Heb. 7:11-16).

Prayer is a necessary part of stoking peace within and making outward change. Once the Apostles approached Jesus and said to him that he should teach them how to pray. His response was a guide or recommendation, NOT a Prayer for repetition as many people do today. The book of Matthew Chapter 6 contains this guide. His main point was to teach us that we should use prayer as a means of obtaining power from God to change ourselves. As God forgives us in Heaven, we should also forgive each other on earth.

Also, the Holy Ghost teaches about praying for material things. He demands that we are not anxious for the things we need from God, but that we should ask and not forget to say thank you even before we receive the response. Any response we receive from God could be Yes or No, but it will always be what is best for us.

> *Be careful for nothing; but in every thing by prayer and supplication with thanksgiving let your requests be made known unto God. And the peace of God, which passeth all understanding, shall keep your hearts and minds through Christ Jesus.* (Phil. 4:6-7).

Prayers are not supposed to be limited to supplications for ourselves. We are responsible for the peace of the lands and nations we inhabit. So the Holy Ghost tells us that there are different styles of praying to God for our temporal leaders and our land:

> *Therefore I exhort first of all that <u>supplications, prayers, intercessions, and giving of thanks</u> be made for all men, for kings and all who are in authority, that we may lead a quiet and peaceable life in all godliness and reverence. For this is good and acceptable in the sight of God our Savior, who desires all men to be saved and to come to the knowledge of the truth. <u>For there is one God and one Mediator between God and men, the Man Christ Jesus</u>, who gave Himself a ransom for all, to be testified in due time* (1 Tim. 2:1-6).

Because you are a part of this One Mediator, you too can intercede on behalf of others.

Above we notice that four different types of prayers are shown to us by the Holy Ghost. <u>Supplications, Prayers, Intercessions, and Giving of Thanks</u>. Generally, all fall under the heading of Prayer, but the purpose and situation should determine which exactly you are using. Supplications mean begging. We usually would be doing this when we are interceding for something or someone that the Holy Ghost has shut the door on. Prayer is when we are generally praying to edify ourselves. *"But ye, beloved, building up yourselves on your most holy faith, praying in the Holy Ghost, "*(Jude. 1:20). Intercession is like supplication but usually directed at a circumstance or spiritual opponent. It is often during an event or before the event. The angel came to Daniel at the time he began to intercede:

Then said he, Knowest thou wherefore I come unto thee? and now will I return to fight with the prince of Persia: and when I am gone forth, lo, the prince of Grecia shall come. But I will shew thee that which is noted in the scripture of truth: and there is none that holdeth with me in these things, but Michael your prince (Dan. 10:20-21).

Giving of thanks is one of the most often overlooked versions of prayer. It often requires the setting aside of time by an individual or group of people to come back and thank God for his answer to prayers, whether he said Yes or No.

The proper relationship between a man and a woman is addressed in several places by the Holy Ghost. It is interesting to note that he hardly ever requires that a woman Love her husband. We only know of one place that alludes to this love, and that, only in passing. It is the man that is required severally by the Holy Ghost to Love his wife. Usually, the Holy Ghost predicates his demands on ability. It seems God expects men to have a greater capability in this area of spousal Love than women. What God demands of women is that they submit to their husband's authority over them:

> *That they may teach the young women to be sober, **to love their husbands**, to love their children, To be discreet, chaste, keepers at home, good, obedient to their own husbands, that the word of God be not blasphemed* (Tit. 2:4-5).

This passage is the only scripture that commands a woman to Love her husband.

This point is crucial to emphasize because too often, based on culture and society, we frequently expect from our spouses, things that God has not required of them. We neglect to give that which is required. In the case of men, God has through the Holy Ghost required that they *Love* and protect their wives. In the case of women, God has through the Holy Ghost required that they *Obey* their husbands.

Due to the contentious nature of modern feminist women against this desire of God, we will give several scriptural examples so that there will no longer be controversy as to what the will of the Holy Ghost is on this matter:

> *Wives submit yourselves unto your own husbands, as unto the Lord. For the husband is the head of the wife, even as Christ is the head of the church: and he is the saviour of the body. <u>Therefore as the church is subject unto Christ, so let the wives be to their own husbands in everything. Husbands, love your wives, even as Christ also loved the church, and gave himself for it:</u> That he might sanctify and cleanse it with the washing of water by the word, That he might present it to himself a glorious church, not having spot, or wrinkle,*

or any such thing; but that it should be holy and without blemish. So ought men to love their wives as their own bodies. He that loveth his wife loveth himself. For no man ever yet hated his own flesh; but nourisheth and cherisheth it, even as the Lord the church: For we are members of his body, of his flesh, and of his bones. For this cause shall a man leave his father and mother, and shall be joined unto his wife, and they two shall be one flesh. This is a great mystery: but I speak concerning Christ and the church. Nevertheless let every one of you in particular so love his wife even as himself; and the wife see that she reverence her husband (Eph. 5:22-33).

The Holy Ghost makes similar demands in Colossians and the book of 1st Peter:

"Wives submit yourselves unto your own husbands, as it is fit in the Lord. Husbands, love your wives, and be not bitter against them" (Col. 3:18-19)) *"Likewise, ye wives, be in subjection to your own husbands; that, if any obey not the word, they also may without the word be won by the conversation of the wives; While they behold your chaste conversation coupled with fear."* (1 Pet. 3:1).

The relationship between a husband and the wife are better if they heed the advice and demands of the Holy Ghost. Unnecessary pain and strife occur when the standards of society determine what a spousal relationship in Christ is. The wife must refer to her husband as "Sir" on occasion *"For after this manner in the old time the holy women also, who trusted in God, adorned themselves, being in subjection unto their own husbands: Even as Sara obeyed Abraham, calling him lord: whose daughters ye are, as long as ye do well, and are not afraid with any amazement"* (1 Pet. 3:6). This reference sets an excellent example for the children who will be able to have a more healthy relationship with their spouses as they develop. It is not demeaning to a woman that her husband is over her. A real wife wants to push her husband to be not only over her but over everything that God has willed to be under him. Also, no husband that believes in Christ wants an unhappy wife. He can derive no pleasure in her sadness, talk less of the fact that his prayers to God become hindered when he makes his wife unhappy. *"Likewise, ye husbands, dwell with them according to knowledge, giving honour unto the wife, as unto the weaker vessel, and as being heirs together of the grace of life; that your prayers be not hindered"* (1 Pet. 3:7).

The Holy Ghost has concerns regarding our attitude and relationships in the workplace. Most of us are unhappy because we find ourselves at "dead-end jobs." This unhappiness is sometimes because of settling for second best, and security, rather than taking the risk to pursue our God-given passions *"Ye lust, and have not: ye kill, and desire to have, and cannot obtain: ye fight and war, yet ye have not, because ye ask not. Ye ask, and receive not, because ye ask amiss, that ye may consume it upon your lusts.* "(Ja. 4:2-3). We settle for second best because we want that new house or car or whatever instead of being patient. Other times we have valid obligations to others like family, that cause us to give up our dreams to take care of them. Whatever the reason, knowing why we have made our choices is better than living a life of grumbling and blaming God. If we had believed God, we would have pursued our dreams and known that God would take care of our responsibilities:

"For the which cause I also suffer these things: nevertheless I am not ashamed: for I know whom I have believed, and am persuaded that he is able to keep that which I have committed unto him against that day" (2 Tim. 1:12). *"I can do all things through Christ which strengtheneth me."* (Phil. 4:13).

No life is a failure. Making money is not evidence of success. Having peace and satisfaction while pursuing your dreams is a success. If necessary, the funds will accompany your accomplishments:

> *But godliness with contentment is great gain. For we brought nothing into this world, and it is certain we can carry nothing out. And having food and raiment let us be therewith content. But they that will be rich fall into temptation and a snare, and into many foolish and hurtful lusts, which drown men in destruction and perdition (1 Tim. 6:6-9).*

Godliness is not just righteous living. It is living a life of satisfaction and understanding that the same Lord who wishes you good health, also wishes you wealth. *"Beloved, I wish above all things that thou mayest prosper and be in health, even as thy soul prospereth "*(3 Jn. 1:2). Most of us have left our passion for something higher, and have run after the god of materialism, through corporate ladder climbing, etc. If we return to God in humility and request a new beginning, we will receive open doors of opportunities. However, we will still need courage if we want to begin pursuing our dreams. *"But the fearful, and unbelieving, and the abominable, and murderers, and whoremongers, and sorcerers, and idolaters, and all liars, shall have their part in the lake which burneth with fire and brimstone: which is the second death "*(Rev. 21:8).

The Holy Ghost is also concerned about our work relationships with our superiors and our subordinates. To our superiors, he expects us to demonstrate humility and respect. Even to those who are obnoxious and undeserving:

> *Servants, be obedient to them that are your masters according to the flesh, with fear and trembling, in singleness of your heart, as unto Christ; Not with eyeservice, as menpleasers; but as the servants of Christ, doing the will of God from the heart; With good will doing service, as to the Lord, and not to men (Eph. 6:5-7).*

Some translations use the word "slave" here; however, that is not the correct translation. The appropriate term is "servants." We know this because the Holy Ghost insists that EVERY worker must be paid wages by his master that is according to the market price for labor:

> *Go to now, ye rich men, weep and howl for your miseries that shall come upon you. Your riches are corrupted, and your garments are motheaten. Your gold and silver is cankered; and the rust of them shall be a witness against you, and shall eat your flesh as it were fire. Ye have heaped treasure together for the last days.* <u>*Behold, the hire of the labourers who have reaped down your fields, which is of you kept back by fraud, crieth: and the cries of them which have reaped are entered into the ears of the Lord of sabaoth.*</u> (Ja. 5:1-4).

This passage demonstrates that the Lord is concerned that we should show regard for those above us, and those that are higher should always be fair to those under them when it comes to compensation.

We have discussed these topics regarding conduct because most of the exhortation of the Holy Ghost to the members of the different assemblies were often to do with decorum. If this were not relevant to our progression toward the Kingdom, he would not emphasize the same points in almost all the different letters through his Apostles. We expect from these points we made, the follower of Christ can begin to alter her attitude toward conduct, both within and without "the household of God."

Next, we will investigate the eschatological dimension of the teachings regarding the "End of Times."

ESCHATOLOGY

T HE "END TIMES" ARE OFTEN DISCUSSED AND WRITTEN ABOUT IN books. In Islam, Judaism, and the Christian Religion, this part of faith is a central article. Therefore, it is necessary that we investigate this subject considering what the scriptures say, and not what very popular mythology and cinematic theatrics have instilled in the minds of people. Certain phrases like *The Beast, The Anti-Christ, Dajjal, New World Order,* etc. are popular phrases to those students of scripture who have eschatology as their main field of study.

The main thrust of belief is that at the end of time, either during, or just before, the Messiah shall return, a personality called The Anti-Christ will rule. This anti-Christ shall turn mankind from worshipping and honoring the true God, to either worshipping himself, or Satan. There will be a great fight between the Anti-Christ and the forces of the Christ, and in the end, Christ shall overcome him. Well, the facts, as set forth by the scriptures, are a bit different from this scenario and contain a lot more subtlety. So, we shall proceed to try and interpret the Apocalypse according to the Grace that the Holy Ghost shall grant us. One thing is certain, *"we must through much Tribulation, enter into the Kingdom of God"* (Acts. 14:22).

The first thing to say is that we are already in the time of the Anti-Christ. Mankind is a kind of spiritual clock. To understand what time we are in the dispensation of the plan of God, all we need to look at is the condition of man. At no time in the known history of mankind did we have the overt and complicit support of the government in the propagation of everything that is forbidden by God. Since the 1990s, it is front-page news about the sexual abuse of minors by catholic priests all over the world, but no large scale national or international public trial of those accused ever takes place. In fact, in most western "democracies," there are organizations legally set up to lobby for the "Rights" of adults to have sexual relations with children legally. One of them in America is named National Men Boys Lovers Association (NAMBLA).

The claim of "liberation" and "freedom" is reversing the traditional roles of spouses. Children are property of the "State," and not primarily the wards of their biological parents. The faith in Jesus Christ now becomes a religion. It was not so in the beginning. Even warfare, which previously we assumed to be a struggle between two armies, is now nothing but a ruse to prop sagging economies by selling military hardware and distracting populations from domestic concerns.

All these things in and of themselves would not be enough to confirm that the anti-Christ is here. However, certain markers laid by the Holy Ghost serve as Leading indicators of the presence of the Anti-Christ. The life of those who profess to believe in Christ serves as the leading indicators.

> *Yet if any man suffer as a Christian, let him not be ashamed; but let him glorify God on this behalf. For the time is come that judgment must begin at the house of God: and if it first begin at us, what shall the end be of them that obey not the gospel of God?* (1 Pet. 4:16-17).

Also, in the letter to Timothy, we read:

> *This know also, that in the last days perilous times shall come. For men shall be lovers of their own selves, covetous, boasters, proud, blasphemers, disobedient to parents, unthankful, unholy, Without natural affection, trucebreakers, false accusers, incontinent, fierce, despisers of those that are good, Traitors, heady, high-minded, lovers of pleasures more than lovers of God; Having a form of godliness, but denying the power thereof: from such turn away* (2 Tim. 3:1-8).

We can see that the description the Holy Ghost gives about people in the last days would not have been unheard of amongst the common people of the time the book was first written. However, it would have been unusual to find such behavior in the Household of God.

> *And the multitude of them that believed were of one heart and of one soul: neither said any of them that ought of the things which he possessed was his own; but they had all things common. And with great power gave the apostles witness of the resurrection of the Lord Jesus: and great grace was upon them all. Neither was there any among them that lacked: for as many as were possessors of lands or houses sold them, and brought the prices of the things that were sold, And laid them down at the apostles' feet: and distribution was made unto every man according as he had need* (Acts. 4:32-33).

These iniquities are now a commonly accepted part of the culture of the Assembly of believers. This acceptance confirms to us that a new god is posing as the true God amid the believers.

> *Now we beseech you, brethren, by the coming of our Lord Jesus Christ, and by our gathering together unto him, That ye be not soon shaken in mind, or be troubled, neither by spirit, nor by word, nor by letter as from us, as that the day of Christ is at hand. Let no man deceive you by any means: for that day shall not come, except there come a falling away first, and that man of sin be revealed, the son of perdition; Who opposeth and exalteth himself above all that is called God, or that is worshipped; so that he as God sitteth in the temple of God, shewing himself that he is God. Remember ye not, that, when I was yet with you, I told you these things?* (2 Thess. 2:1-5).

The Holy Ghost says in this scripture that he would "sit in the Temple." What does this mean? Will we build a new physical temple? Not according to scripture. The only temple being built, and which exists in spirit is the Body of Believers. Therefore, the Holy Ghost is saying WITHIN the Assembly; a strong delusion shall grip the majority of believers and the world to think that the doctrines that they are receiving are the doctrines of Christ. The intent is to neutralize the efficacy of the true Word of God that has the power to transform.

Speaking about the temple, we had earlier said the natural temple had three courts. Well, the spiritual temple also has three courts: our spirits, souls, and bodies. Remember, the spiritual temple is the body of believers, not a physical building. The Holy Ghost tells us in Revelation, chapter 11:

> *And there was given me a reed like unto a rod: and the angel stood, saying, Rise, and measure the temple of God, and the altar, and them that worship therein. <u>But the court which is without the temple leave out, and measure it not; for it is given unto the Gentiles:</u> and the holy city shall they tread under foot forty and two month* (Rev. 11:1-2).

The Apostle John was shown the Assembly in the spirit and asked to measure them. He saw the people as a temple with three parts but was told NOT to measure those in the third part, the outer Court, because "Gentiles" had been allowed to trample upon it for "forty-two months." This scripture informs us that at the end of time, spiritually uncircumcised persons and the work of the flesh will have access to an aspect of the

Assembly, hence the use of the phrase "Gentiles." No doubt, the occurrences in the Assemblies today point to a particular spiritual decline among us.

The very first verse in the book of Revelation says, *"This is the Revelation of Jesus Christ, which God gave to him, to <u>show his disciples</u> things which must shortly come to pass and he sent and signified it by his angel unto his servant John"* (Rev. 1:1). This passage means that everything we read in Revelations is futuristic. It was pointing toward something or some time to come. In our search for understanding of the Kingdom, the book of Revelation is a necessary component of the puzzle. Understanding its coded nuances require a mastery and initiation into the symbolic language used to conceal from the uninvited, the wonderful mystery of the Kingdom.

In the 11th Chapter of Revelation, we see the Holy Ghost describe his "two witnesses" who would elucidate the message of the Kingdom during a set number of days. *"And I will give power unto my two witnesses, and they shall prophesy a thousand two hundred and threescore days clothed in sackcloth"* (Rev. 11:3). What is significant about the number of days is that it corresponds to the same *forty-two months* we read earlier in which the Gentiles would tread upon the outer court that ought not to be measured. Also significant is that forty-two months adds up to three and a half years. The exact number of years that Jesus spent doing his ministry work. This number, three and a half, on its own has no significance in scripture outside the fact that Elijah's withholding of Rain over Israel lasted the same length of time. The number comes alive if we recognize Jesus' ministry as being cut short according to the predetermined plan of God and that when added to the ministry of the "Two witnesses," we have a total of SEVEN years of ministry. Seven is our number for perfection.

Now, to simplify this matter, we need to know that the "two witnesses" are not a literal two people. They represent symbolically the two Israelites who were the only ones to enter the promised land under Joshua, due to their tenacity and obedience to God; Joshua and Caleb. These "two witnesses" are the Elect followers of Christ who not only come out from the world but also make it into the Kingdom. The ministry of Jesus AND that of the two witnesses are the fulfillment of the scriptures that say, *"LET US make man in our image"* and *"For we are labourers together with God: ye are God's husbandry, ye are God's building"* (1 Cor. 3:9). Jesus began the work of making us into the Image AND Likeness of God, but the two witnesses through the hands of the Holy Ghost, are going to be the persons to complete the molding of the Elect into Christ:

"My little children, of whom I travail in birth again until Christ be formed in you" (Gal. 4:19). *"Yea doubtless, and I count all things but loss for the excellency of the knowledge of Christ Jesus my*

Lord: for whom I have suffered the loss of all things, and do count them but dung, **that I may win Christ**" (Phil. 3:8).

As we go deeper into the Apocalypse, we would like to remind you that this book has a clear intention. The intention is to make more understandable, the pathway to the Kingdom of God, and what exactly this means. As a reminder, we began this book by stating that YOU are the Kingdom of God. We said that you are not yet ready to be fully inhabited by God and that everything going on, in and around you are programmed to bring you into the place of preparation for transformation into a habitation for God. If you continue to remember this as we dissect the meat of the Word in the eschatology, you will begin to see clearly how your transformation is the central theme of the book of Revelation.

The apocalypse begins with an admonition to the assemblies from Christ through his Apostle, John. While he has varying degrees of admonishments for each assembly, he traditionally ends these with a promise to reward those who overcome. *"To him that overcometh will I grant to sit with me in my throne, even as I also overcame, and am set down with my Father in his throne"* (Rev. 3:21). Secondly, he tells the apostle to inform the assemblies that he is standing outside of their hearts and knocking. *"Behold, I stand at the door, and knock: if any man hear my voice, and open the door, I will come in to him, and will sup with him, and he with me* "(Rev. 3:20). These statements, which we know are for those who have already become believers in Christ. The statements admonish the believer to strive to attain something more. What is that thing? After all, they already have salvation:

> *Unto me, who am less than the least of all saints, is this grace given, that I should preach among the Gentiles the unsearchable riches of Christ; And to make all men see what is the fellowship of the mystery, which from the beginning of the world hath been hid in God, who created all things by Jesus Christ:* **To the intent that now unto the principalities and powers in heavenly places might be known by the church the manifold wisdom of God,** *According to the eternal purpose which he purposed in Christ Jesus our Lord: In whom we have boldness and access with confidence by the faith of him* (Eph. 3:8-12).

The book of Philippians quotes the great Apostle Paul as confessing that he had not yet ATTAINED the Status, which he believed he received a calling to attain. Does this mean he was not worthy of entering the spiritual realm of God at his physical death? Obviously not. But to what exactly was he alluding?

In the fourth chapter of Revelation, John the Revelator tells us this:

> *After this I looked, and there before me was a door standing open in heaven. And the voice I had first heard speaking to me like a trumpet said, "Come up here, and I will show you what must take place after this." At once I was in the Spirit, and there before me was a throne in heaven with someone sitting on it. And the one who sat there had the appearance of jasper and ruby. A rainbow that shone like an emerald encircled the throne. Surrounding the throne were* **twenty-four other thrones and seated on them were twenty-four elders**. *They were dressed in white and had crowns of gold on their heads. From the throne came flashes of lightning, rumblings and peals of thunder. In front of the throne, seven lamps were blazing. These are the seven spirits of God. Also, in front of the throne there was what looked like a sea of glass, clear as crystal. In the center, around the throne, were four living creatures, and they were covered with eyes, in front and in back.* **The first living creature was like a lion, the second was like an ox, the third had a face like a man, the fourth was like a flying eagle** (Rev. 4:1-7).

The twenty-four elders represent the earthly and heavenly priesthood who are continually in an attitude of prayer concerning the welfare of mankind and the development of God's work in man. It is not a literal number. It was foreshadowed in the Old Testament by the twenty-four descendants of Aaron the High Priest through his sons Eleazar and Ithamar when King David recognized them as the priests of God (1 Chronicles 23:1-19). They are men and women who have given themselves to the cause of the transformation of man through reconciliation to God. The four living creatures (four beasts) represent the four dimensions of the soul of man. The Lion is symbolic of our Emotions, the Ox (Calf) is symbolic of our Will, the Man is symbolic of our Desire, and the Eagle is symbolic of our Mind (see Ezekiel chapter 11). These are not four creatures, but one. It is important to note two important distinctions between the same Beasts in Ezekiel and Revelation. In Revelation, due to the transformative work done in the souls of believers, the Ox of Ezekiel has been transformed into a Calf (Signifying a more malleable Will). While the Eagle in Ezekiel has been transformed into a Flying Eagle (Signifying a spiritual Mind). All these are esoteric indicators of the transformative work of God through the sacrifice of Christ.

As we mentioned at the beginning of this book, Man is a soul, he lives in a body, and he has a spirit. The spirit of all men is weak relative to the body at the time of birth. The body craves things that are superficial and transient, while the spirit craves things that are esoteric and spiritual. The life of Jesus in man's soul is the only way a soul can ascend. The holy spirit accelerates this ascension by infusing the soul with power. *"And fear not them which kill the body, but are not able to kill the soul: but rather fear him which is able to destroy both soul and body in hell "*(Matt. 10:28). The soul is pulled continually in one direction or the other. By using the power of words and faith, God saves the soul by calling out to God through Christ for help, *"For whosoever shall call upon the name of the Lord shall be saved. How then shall they call on him in whom they have not believed? and how shall they believe in him of whom they have not heard? and how shall they hear without a preacher? "*(Rom. 10:13-14).

Therefore, we see the four Beasts singing praises to the person sitting on the throne and proclaiming that he had saved them. These could not be Angels, and neither could it have been natural animals. The only creature that we know can praise Christ for salvation is Man.

In the fifth chapter of the Revelation, we see a scenario in which the revelator sees a dilemma concerning a book that was closed because no one was found worthy enough to open it. The revelator was saddened and about to cry when one of the twenty-four elders walked up and told him not to cry because "the Lamb" had been found worthy of opening the book. What is the meaning of this vision, and how does it apply to our quest for the kingdom?

The book is an esoteric form of describing a life:

> *And I saw the dead, small and great, stand before God; and the books were opened: and another book was opened, which is the book of life: and the dead were judged out of those things which were written in the books, according to their works. And the sea gave up the dead which were in it; and death and hell delivered up the dead which were in them: and they were judged every man according to their works. And death and hell were cast into the lake of fire. This is the second death. And whosoever was not found written in the book of life was cast into the lake of fire* (Rev. 20:12-15).

The book that no one could open is symbolic of your life and the struggles and joys you have experienced in it. You and I cannot save ourselves from our dilemmas, but the Lamb of God can. After this scene, the revelator sees the future in which different colored horses and horsemen upon release accomplish some work of punishment on the earth. Included in these punishments are health pandemics and economic hardships. These punishments are meted out to us out of love, with an intent to get us to ask ourselves where we are going with our destiny. However, the revelator sees that even these will not stop mankind from continuing to persevere in wickedness, witchcraft, and murder:

And the rest of the men which were not killed by these plagues yet repented not of the works of their hands, that they should not worship devils, and idols of gold, and silver, and brass, and stone, and of wood: which neither can see, nor hear, nor walk: Neither repented they of their murders, nor of their sorceries, nor of their fornication, nor of their thefts (Rev. 9:20-21).

In the seventh chapter, we see that while these things are going on, the Lord would send his "Angels" out to SEAL the believers and protect them from the spiritual effects of these calamities. The angels here who do the sealing are men, not spirits. The number of people given as being sealed by the "angels" is 144,000. This figure is not a literal number. It is just symbolic of the believers who had their way of mind and thinking altered from the current state of thinking by most people around them. This change of mind and thinking can transform people both spiritually and physically. *"And be not conformed to this world: but be ye transformed by the renewing of your mind, that ye may prove what is that good, and acceptable, and perfect, will of God."* (Rom. 12:2).

Friends, this period in which we live in the time spoken about in Revelation. We are living during the great tribulation, and we pray that we might not drawback once the persecution becomes tougher. Many of us have put our hope in economic and political systems. We see our country or nation as better or safer than the next. The truth is that different fires are burning around us. While economic and political repression might be overtly occurring someplace else, right where you are, an even more insidious fire is burning around you. Your children are being transformed into sexual demons by "Hollywood" and "Music," but you cannot stop them. Your spouse is no longer excited about spirituality and the pursuit of the Kingdom. He or she has settled for the feel-good messages from the modern millionaire pastors. Your prayer and fasting life erode consistently, and you are overwhelmed with loans and mortgages. All these are signs of the End. You must remember what was said to the seven assemblies at the beginning of the Revelation; *"to he that overcomes."* You might not be able to save all whom you love, but God will give every one of them a means of escape. Inform them about it and go your way.

These events occurring on the outside are a consequence of what is taking place inside the Assemblies. Once we believed in the message of the Kingdom, we became implanted with the seed of God. This process is the spiritual correlation of a woman receiving sperm from a man. The fact that she has received his sperm is no guarantee that she will conceive, neither give birth. As you might know, when sperm enter into a female, there might be millions searching for her egg. They must travel to where her egg is, but only as few as six might arrive at the area of the egg. The egg emits an odor that attracts the sperm. The sperm releases some proteins that allow it to enter the egg, and thereby fertilize it from within. Once one of the sperms is inside, the egg develops a barricade that stops any other sperm from getting in. Then begins the process of development of a child, as when Christ enters your life. *"Blessed be the God and Father of our Lord Jesus Christ, who hath blessed us with all spiritual blessings in heavenly places in Christ"* (Eph. 1:13).

Since you have received the Word of Christ, now you are impregnated with his son. Your life is about managing this pregnancy to full term, and not letting any accident or malice abort the child. Therefore, the Holy Ghost tells us *"my children for whom I am in pains, until Christ is formed in you"* (Gal. 4:19), and in another place, *"Christ in you, the hope of glory"* (Col. 1:27). These and other scriptures indicate that we began a pregnancy when we received the truth of Christ.

In the twelfth chapter of the Revelation, we see another scenario in which a pregnant woman having a crown of twelve stars, and the moon under her feet, is in labor and about to give birth:

> *And there appeared a great wonder in heaven; a woman clothed with the sun, and the moon under her feet, and upon her head a crown of twelve stars:* ***And she being with child cried, travailing in birth, and pained to be delivered****. And there appeared another wonder in heaven; and behold a great red dragon, having seven heads and ten horns, and seven crowns upon his heads. And his tail drew the third part of the stars of heaven and did cast them to the earth: and the dragon stood before the woman which was ready to be delivered, for to devour her child as soon as it was born. And she brought forth a man child, who was to rule all nations with a rod of iron: and her* ***child was caught up unto God****, and to his throne. And the woman fled into the wilderness, where she hath a place prepared of God, that they should feed her there a thousand two hundred and threescore days* (Rev. 12:1-6).

This woman is symbolic of people who receive and hold this message until the end, who overcome every obstacle put in their way thru the Holy Spirit. Your studying of this book is an excellent armor for you towards this goal. Let us briefly discuss the symbolism of this vision.

First, we need to know that this imagery is not of an individual but concerning an Assembly of believers. The twelve stars around her head are symbolic of an apostolic and divine headship over our mind. Her pregnancy is the birthing of the "Sons of God" in the period of the end. *"For the earnest expectation of the creature waiteth for the manifestation of the sons of God. "*(Rom. 8:19).

The sun around her designates her as the chosen assembly (church), while the moon **UNDER** her feet shows us the state of the rejected assembly (church). The rejected assembly is not only at a lower level, but the sun is shining on the woman, and not the moon. The moon no longer reflects the glory of the sun; it is the woman that does. She gives birth to a **MAN CHILD**, not a male child. This wording means he is a bone as an adult. This birth takes place in the heavenly realm, where the woman obviously resides. However, the scriptures tell us that he, the man child, is "caught up" to God. If he was born in heaven, how can he again be caught up to God? It is figurative but suggests that there are multiple heavens. He exercises his power in a realm that is higher than that of his mother. Who is his mother? The glorious church. Who is he? The Elect of God whom we have spoken about several times in previous chapters. The sons of God. Not just one individual.

The dragon that waits to devour her child is Satan, as expressed on earth through the unrighteous political systems in alliance with the religious system and false prophets teaching lies in the name of God (Is. 9:15). They operate as agents of a spiritual force ready to destroy the sons, just as Herod once tried to destroy the baby, Jesus. The dragon had seven heads and ten horns, which indicates to us that this is the residue of the ten toes of Nebuchadnezzar's image, as we read earlier in Daniel. *"And whereas thou sawest the feet and toes, part of potters' clay, and part of iron, the kingdom shall be divided; but there shall be in it of the strength of the iron, forasmuch as thou sawest the iron mixed with miry clay. "*(Dan. 2:41).

The seven heads symbolizing that they have a divine mandate for a time, and the ten horns symbolizing rule by a group of men during this period:

> Let every soul be subject unto the higher powers. For there is no power but of God: the powers that be are ordained of God. Whosoever therefore resisteth the power, resisteth the ordinance of God: and they that resist shall receive to themselves damnation. For rulers are not a terror to good works, but to the evil. Wilt thou then not be afraid of the power? do that which is good, and thou shalt have praise of the same: For he is the minister of God

to thee for good. But if thou do that which is evil, be afraid; for he beareth not the sword in vain: for he is the minister of God, a revenger to execute wrath upon him that doeth evil. Wherefore ye must needs be subject, not only for wrath, but also for conscience sake. For for this cause pay ye tribute also: for they are God's ministers, attending continually upon this very thing (Rom. 13:1-6).

It is noteworthy that Revelation says that she gave birth to A son. We know that Jesus has already been born and that the very first verse in the book of Revelation tells us that all the visions John would be shown concerned the future (Rev. 1:1). Therefore, this child she gave birth to cannot be Jesus, because he was already born in the past by Mary in the manger. In addition to the fact that the "woman" is spiritual and not an individual. she escapes from the dragon after giving birth to an adult (Man Child) who is to rule the universe. (It says MAN CHILD, not Male child). However, there will be a period of contention before this adult takes control of the world. Here again, we meet that number, three and a half years (one thousand two hundred and threescore days).

As we mentioned before, the world is currently in the time of the Tribulation spoken about by Jesus and Daniel the prophet. With so-called smart-phones and the internet, there is no corner of the globe now that the gospel of Jesus cannot reach. Even the communists in China have given up trying to stop the inflow of the gospel, and the Soviet Union is no more. In the Islamic nations, people have access to the Gospel of the Kingdom readily available on their handsets. The only thing that is in short supply today is people with boldness and conviction to testify within the so-called "free world" about its impending destruction.

Many in Europe and America have taken for granted the freedom and liberty they received through the prayers of their forefathers and mothers, that suffered deprivation and religious oppression. Western society has become the arch-enemy of God. Even the city that bears the name Jerusalem today has a government-sanctioned "Gay" Homosexual parade each year. These abominable practices are justified as "freedom of expression" without regard to the moral influence on children who do not yet know Right from Wrong. At no other time in human history has the whole world been cajoled into such acquiescence to ungodliness.

America, Europe, and the country today referred to as Israel has become the right arm of Satan upon the earth. The leaders of these nations have used the leadership granted them by the grace of God to teach abomination throughout the world. Abortion of innocent children in the mother's womb they call "Choice." The separation of fathers from their homes based on the whims of unfaithful women is considered a virtue. There's no consideration for the spiritual, psychological, and moral impact on any children left behind. It is not for nothing that God threatened to smite the earth with a curse because of this very act:

> *Behold, I will send you Elijah the prophet before the coming of the great and dreadful day of the LORD: And he shall turn the heart of the fathers to the children, and the heart of the children to their fathers, lest I come and smite the earth with a curse* (Mal. 4:5-6).

No nation or persons that have contributed directly or indirectly to these abominations shall escape the wrath that is coming. Those of us who live in such nations should prepare for the wrath that is to come upon us.

At the end of time, there will be a spiritual war between men and Satan for control of the "aura" of mankind. The aura is the realm that the bible refers to as "Air." This realm is from where Satan currently rules the souls of men. This realm is the reason why we refer to him as the Prince of the power of the air (Eph. 2:2). This battle will be led by Jesus when he comes down from heaven to *meet with us* in the realm called "Air" (1 Thess. 4:17). In the twelfth chapter of Revelation, the imagery used by God to describe this event is one in which Michael *and* his Angels fight against the Serpent and defeat him:

> *And there was war in heaven: Michael and his angels fought against the dragon; and the dragon fought and his angels, And prevailed not; neither was their place found any more in heaven. And the great dragon was cast out, that old serpent, called the Devil, and Satan, which deceiveth the whole world: he was cast out into the earth, and his angels were cast out with him* (Rev. 12:7-9).

The imagery here is of the same event we see occurring in the fourth chapter of 1Thessalonians, where it says we get caught up to meet the lord in the air. It is a spiritual event, not a physical one. It leads to a confrontation with the ruler of the Air. The angels described who fight with Michael against the dragon are the Christians. We know so because it says they overcame the Dragon <u>by the blood of Jesus and their testimony</u>. Spirit angels do not have a testimony. *"And they overcame him by the blood of the Lamb, and by the word of their testimony; and they loved not their lives unto the death"* (Rev. 12:11).

This "birthing" of a Man Child by the "woman" symbolizes the fulfillment Romans chapter eight:

For the earnest expectation of the creature **waiteth for the manifestation of the sons of God**. *For the creature was made subject to vanity, not willingly, but by reason of him who hath subjected the same in hope, Because the creature itself also shall be delivered from the bondage of corruption into the glorious liberty of the children of God. For we know that the whole creation groaneth and travaileth in pain together until now. And not only they, but ourselves also, which have the firstfruits of the Spirit, even we ourselves groan within ourselves, waiting for the adoption, to wit, the redemption of our body* (Rom. 8:19-23).

Can you see the correspondence between Revelation 12 and Romans 8? While the Holy Ghost tells us in the book of Romans that their will come a "manifestation" of the sons of God, the book of Revelation shows a vision of ONE person being born by the woman. This vision hearkens back to what we had seen earlier in Daniel 7 when he saw the Son of man being led to the "Ancient of Days" to receive Glory. The angel interpreted the vision for Daniel by telling him that the individual was a group of people. *"And the kingdom and dominion, and the greatness of the kingdom under the whole heaven, shall be given to the people of the saints of the Most High, whose kingdom is an everlasting kingdom, and all dominions shall serve and obey him* "(Dan. 7:27).

This manifestation of the sons of God, or the birthing of the Man Child will occur by a singular act of physiological and psychological transformation:

Behold, I shew you a mystery; We shall not all sleep, **but we shall all be changed**, *In a moment, in the twinkling of an eye, at the last trump: for the trumpet shall sound, and the dead shall be raised incorruptible, and we shall be changed. For this corruptible must put on incorruption, and this mortal must put on immortality* (1 Cor. 15:51-53).

Just as Satan sought to devour the baby Moses and the baby Jesus, he shall seek to devour the Sons of God at our manifestation. He will do this because he knows that this physiological and psychological change that will affect the "Elect" will cause the eventual end of his rule of unrighteousness on earth. The battle is for the souls and bodies of people because, without our bodies, no Spirit can adequately function within the material realm. That is why there is a "body of Christ." It is the body by which God can function in the material realm. It is a body that has no beginning and has no end. *"Sacrifice and offering thou didst not desire; mine ears hast thou opened: burnt offering and sin offering hast thou not required. Then said I, Lo, I come: in the volume of the book it is written of me* "(Ps. 40:6-7).

Wherefore when he cometh into the world, he saith, Sacrifice and offering thou wouldest not, but a body hast thou prepared me: In burnt offerings and sacrifices for sin thou hast had no pleasure. Then said I, Lo, I come (in the volume of the book it is written of me,) to do thy will, O God. Above when he said, Sacrifice and offering and burnt offerings and offering for sin thou wouldest not, neither hadst pleasure therein; which are offered by the law; Then said he, Lo, I come to do thy will, O God. He taketh away the first, that he may establish the second (Heb. 10:5-9).

This quotation in the bible book of Hebrews is by the Holy Ghost, drawing from the original in Psalms. We can see from the quote in Hebrews that the Body of Christ, which God invites us to partake in, existed from the foundation of time. God offers us the privilege to be a part of it. The fact that you are in the assembly/church does not necessarily mean that you are in the body of Christ. That is not to say you are not a Christian/Believer. May God give us wisdom concerning this. To be in the body of Christ suggests that you have now entered the second part of the Tabernacle called the Holy Place. You no longer depend on the natural Sunlight to see. You now use the Seven Golden Lampstands as your source of light. This relationship esoterically means that you don't depend on human impulse and human reasoning to determine wrong from right, or what the will of God is. You move by Revelation from the Holy Ghost most of the time.

What is often called the "Rapture" should more appropriately be called the "Ressurection." Now, we can see clearly that the rapture is not an event in which we shall physically leave this world into the sky, but an event in which we shall be "changed" in this world, with a new heavenly nature. It is this change in nature that the Holy Ghost euphemistically refers to as being "Caught Up":

For the Lord himself shall descend from heaven with a shout, with the voice of the archangel, and with the trump of God: and the dead in Christ shall rise first: Then we which are alive and remain <u>shall be caught up</u> together with them in the clouds, to meet the Lord in the air: and so shall we ever be with the Lord (1 Thess. 4:16-17).

An exoteric reading of scripture has blinded many to the simplicity of the scriptures regarding the sons of God. This "caught up" is NOT a geographical direction, but rather a qualitative direction. God shall lift us from this carnal nature of temptation and mortality to one that is indestructible and immune to sin. We shall obtain the same kind of body that Jesus had after the resurrection. "*Who shall <u>change our vile body</u>, that it may* *be fashioned like unto his glorious body, according to the working whereby he is able even to subdue all things unto himself"* (Phil. 3:21).

This transformation is what it means to be in the Kingdom of God. To be saved is a gift of God that comes from believing in the saving work of Jesus Christ. It is not our effort that saves us. It is free. However, to enter the Kingdom, we need to be co-laborers with God working out our salvation, to be found worthy to enter the Kingdom. Not entering the Kingdom does not mean you have lost your salvation. However, it means you have not been pleasing to God. You will never lose your salvation except you lose your faith in Jesus Christ. For *"many are called, but few are chosen"* (Matt. 22:14). The word "called" in the bible is the Greek word "Ecclesia." It is the word translated "Church" or "Assembly."

A message to children:

Children are under the most dangerous spiritual threats since the beginning of recorded time. Cyberbullying, inappropriate sexual images, broken homes, and outright physical violence are snuffing out the innocence of children. The devil seeks to destroy children because they are the ones who are most dangerous to his kingdom. They do not get easily distracted by the allure of the world until Satan teaches them so. The world introduces phenomena to distract children.

Satan intends these phenomena to destroy children and make them captive for the Kingdom of Darkness and its agents here. All children must know that God sees them and desires that they call out to him for help and deliverance. As a child, you might say, "if God was so kind and loving, why does he have to wait for me to ask him for help?" The answer is not complicated.

Long before you were born, our first ancestors ceded control of this world to Satan. Satan exists as the power behind the wickedness on earth. Since God gave our ancestors the power over everything in this world, he cannot take it back. The principles upon which God created the Universe does not permit him to interfere in our lives without our express permission. Once he has given something to you, he does not take it back. *"For the gifts and calling of God are without repentance"* (Romans 11:29)

There is hope, however. Now because of Jesus Christ and his willingness to give up his own perfect life for us, you can call on him to deliver you from any situation or circumstance with which you find yourself entangled. Just test what I have said and see if you do not begin to experience a change in your condition. No person who calls on the name of Jesus does not receive and answer from him.

The devil intends to get you hooked on alcohol and drugs because he knows that when you do not have a sound mind, you are subject to manipulation and control by his forces. He also wants to use indoctrination of the educational system to pull down your moral standing. Go to school, learn your subjects, but do not receive your morals of what is Right or Wrong from your teachers. You must receive that from your parents. Even if your parents are immoral, they will not want you to follow an immoral path. Teachers teach you because they get money for the job. Your parents teach you because God has put a love in them for you. *"Honor your father and Mother that your days may be long"* (Exodus 20:12). God also tells your parents not to make you bitter or extremely sad because he loves you. *"And ye fathers, provoke not your children to wrath; but bring them up in the nurture and admonition of the Lord"* (Ephesians 6:4)

Do unto others whatever you would like others to do unto you. Please do not laugh at other children because they have a disability. God allowed you to see that so you can have an opportunity to be kind to someone. It is a test from God. When you are on a bus, and you see a much older person standing, offer your seat to them, and you will be surprised how other people will give you gifts in your life.

Never raise your voice rudely at adults, especially your parents. If you dishonor your mother and father, you might have a short life or an unfulfilled life. Your parents are like angels. They might not be the best, but God chose them for a reason. When you are very successful in life, and people only tell you what you want to hear, it is your parents that will tell you the truth that you might not want to hear. Your parents are very important.

Respect your older siblings and be extra kind to your younger brothers and sisters. Many of them will annoy you sometimes, but remember God put you in their lives because they need you. They might not know your value to them, but God does. Whenever you go to sleep angry at them, remember to ask God to help you forgive them before you sleep. *"Whoever hates his brother is a murderer, and you know that no murderer has eternal life abiding in him"* (1 John 3:15)

Many adults have emotional and psychological problems so they can hurt innocent children who are trusting of strangers. Do not trust any stranger who you do know. Family friends should not be allowed into your home if your parents are not home. The only exception is if your parents explicitly told you that family, friends, or relatives are coming over.

Watch videos about your school work and about any subject you like in school. It helps you get a good picture of what you want to be in the future. Read about the lives of the people who are doing what you would like to do. Maybe you want to be a Doctor, a soldier, a scientist, or a business billionaire. Read about the lives of these people, and you will become like them. Most people become like the person they admire the most.

Start saving money in a safe place, even if it is only pennies. As time goes on, you will find that you have saved enough to invest in shares of companies that make some of the things you like. You will become a young shareholder. All these things I am sharing with you are what God likes. He loves seeing children behave responsibly and emulate Jesus.

There is no limit to what you can achieve if you call on Jesus to guide you. In the bible, he says the Kingdom of God belongs to people who are like children. Always remain friendly and respectful. Hold no grudges or bitterness toward your friends. Be truthful as much as you can be. Lies are the work of Satan. Do not be a liar.

Remember that God is love and that he says that whoever touches you, touches his Iris. *"For thus says the Lord of Hosts; After the Glory hath he sent me unto the nations which spoilt you, for he that toucheth you, toucheth the Apple of his eye"* (Zecharia 2:8)

NEW HEAVEN, NEW EARTH

P REVIOUSLY WE DESCRIBED THE TRANSFORMATION THAT WILL take place in the physiological and psychological makeup of those who do not receive the "Mark of the Beast" (the Mark of the Beast on the forehead or arm is symbolic of the transformation of the mind and acts of people from righteousness to unrighteousness). Those who resist Satan to the end are the people who will be given the natural reins of earthly Government for a period often referred to as the "Millennium." This period is not necessarily a literal one-thousand-year rule. The number is significant as it refers to the seed of God, Christ. The people found worthy to enter the Kingdom will rule with Christ:

> *And I saw thrones, and they sat upon them, and judgment was given unto them: and I saw the souls of them that were beheaded for the witness of Jesus, and for the word of God, and which had not worshipped the beast, neither his image, neither had received his mark upon their foreheads, or in their hands; and they lived and reigned with Christ a thousand years* (Rev. 20:4).

During our rule, there will be peace on earth and no more wars as we have them today. However, people will still be going after their business as they do today. Planting and harvesting, enjoying sports, etc. but there will not be the fear and chaos to the extent that we have today. However, after a period, Satan (after being loosed from the bottomless pit) will instigate people on earth to be contentious about our rule:

> *And when the thousand years are expired, Satan shall be loosed out of his prison, And shall go out to deceive the nations which are in the four quarters of the earth, Gog and Magog, to gather them together to battle: the number of whom is as the sand of the sea. And they went up on the breadth of the earth, and compassed the camp of the saints about, and the beloved city: and fire came down from God out of heaven, and devoured them. And the devil that*

deceived them was cast into the lake of fire and brimstone, where the beast and the false prophet are, and shall be tormented day and night for ever and ever (Rev. 20:7-10).

The profiteers of this current suffering dispensation will be able to provoke some of the masses to seek to rebel against our rule.

This expression of ingratitude will provoke the ultimate wrath of God, and he will send a terrible judgment on the earth at this time. It will provoke the war of Gog and Magog as prophesied by Ezekiel. It is important to note that all this is taking place AFTER the 1000 year "reign of Christ." A lot of scholars erroneously assume that these two entities are referring to some of our current countries. There is no evidence of that from this chronology.

After this rebellion, all the Christians who did not make it into the 1000 years "the reign of Christ," and all other dead people will stand before the *Great White Throne* for the final Judgment. God will bring out for Judgment, even those in Hell. Only the persons whose names are in a particular book will be saved and allowed into the New Heaven and New Earth. That book is a peculiar life, the life of Christ. A life of sacrifice. God will cast all others into the *Lake of Fire*. Note that Hell is not the Lake of Fire:

> *And I saw a great white throne, and him that sat on it, from whose face the earth and the heaven fled away; and there was found no place for them. And I saw the dead, small and great, stand before God; and the books were opened: and another book was opened, which is the book of life: and the dead were judged out of those things which were written in the books, according to their works. And the sea gave up the dead which were in it; and death and hell delivered up the dead which were in them: and they were judged every man according to their works. And death and hell were cast into the lake of fire. This is the second death. And whosoever was not found written in the book of life was cast into the lake of fire.* (Rev. 20:11-15).

Hell is a state of permanent separation from God, filled with emotional and physical pain and regret.

After the final judgment, a transformation will occur in the physiology of every living thing. This transformation will be the fulfillment of the third and final feast. The feast of Tabernacles. When God, in the person of Jesus Christ, makes earth his permanent abode. The bible describes this event as the coming down of the Heavenly Jerusalem, the bride of Christ:

And I saw a new heaven and a new earth: for the first heaven and the first earth were passed away; and there was no more sea. And I John saw the holy city, new Jerusalem, coming down from God out of heaven, prepared as a bride adorned for her husband. And I heard a great voice out of heaven saying, Behold, the tabernacle of God is with men, and he will dwell with them, and they shall be his people, and God himself shall be with them, and be their God (Rev. 21:1-3).

We do not have much clarity as of now about exactly how the universe shall be when the Heavenly Jerusalem is manifest in creation, but we do have some insight into the thousand-year reign of Christ. We will explore that a little here, but we must do a little review of what we have learned so far.

We said that the intention of God in creating man was to have a home in which to dwell, to have someone with which he could have a personal relationship. A person with free will. To have an avenue to express his Love, and to manifest the Kingdom of God in the natural Universe.

To accomplish this, he needed to make man, not only in his Image but also in his Likeness. Making man in his image was an immediate act that entailed simply forming him from dust and breathing into his nostrils. However, making man into his Likeness required a long process. We said that process is still ongoing, and God will accomplish this at the heralding of the last trumpet:

Behold, I shew you a mystery; We shall not all sleep, but we shall all be changed, In a moment, in the twinkling of an eye, at the last trump: for the trumpet shall sound, and the dead shall be raised incorruptible, and we shall be changed (1 Cor. 15:51-52).

The making of man into the likeness of God is a mystery hidden even now to the uninitiated. When we read the scripture talking about Trumpets sounding, it is an esoteric message that the unveiling of a mystery is now occurring. This change is why in Thessalonians and Revelation, we read the "mystery" of God is coming to an end at the sound of the last trumpet:

Even the mystery which hath been hid from ages and from generations, but now is made manifest to his saints: To whom God would make known what is the riches of the glory of this mystery among the Gentiles; which is Christ in you, the hope of glory (Col.1:26-27).

We said man fell from a level of confidence in God when he listened to his wife and ate from a tree that God had told him not to eat. The Serpent deceived the wife, and she persuaded her husband to do other than that which God had commanded him. Even though God was willing to continue his fellowship with the Man, the man himself was unable to and was constantly afraid of God's presence. He would flee at the sound of God's footsteps (*It is so today for every soul that dies after rejecting Jesus Christ*). Therefore, God decided to help man by putting him away from his presence until God restored man's conscience by the offering of Jesus Christ.

We said that even though God is Love, he also is a God of Justice. He could not just manifest in the world as a human being to save mankind without being prepared to risk his essence, subjecting himself to the elements, subject to the Law, because he had given the universe to man, and the "accuser" was standing by to point out a flaw. If God were to save man, he would need the "*locus standi*" to do so. He was given that Right by Abraham's obedience when he was willing to sacrifice Isaac for God. This act of Abraham allowed God to offer his Self in the person of his Son, Jesus Christ This meant he would have to pay for the mistake of man "out of his own pocket." The Law of God states that the soul that sins must die; therefore, God could not save any soul without intervening. If he intervened as God, that would be unjust to the other spirits that faced eternal damnation. To save mankind and be Just at the same time, God had to come in the weakness of a human being: tempted in every way Satan tempts you and more. He had to come in the form of a human being. "*For we have not an high priest which cannot be touched with the feeling of our infirmities; but was in all points tempted like as we are, yet without sin*" (Heb. 4:15).

Therefore, he chose Abraham as a person to offer the deal of eternal friendship. Depending on Abraham's attitude towards God, God would be obligated to have a special relationship with him. Due to the understanding of covenants then held by peoples and their gods, this would be one that transferred from one generation to another. When Abraham was tested by God to offer his "only son," he did not flinch in obeying God. However, God stopped him from carrying out the act and declared that because of Abraham's obedience, going forward, God would always keep his covenant with Abraham's seed, not seeds. "*Now to Abraham and his seed were the promises made. He saith not, And to seeds, as of many; but as of one, And to thy seed, which is Christ*" (Gal. 3:16). This act of Abraham opened the portal, making God justified in saving the seed of Abraham from any future destruction. So now, anyone in Christ who is Abraham's seed has full access to all the benefits of Abraham AND Christ.

And the scripture, foreseeing that God would justify the heathen through faith, preached before the gospel unto Abraham, saying, In thee shall all nations be blessed. So then they which be of faith are blessed with faithful Abraham. For as many as are of the works of the law are under the curse: for it is written, Cursed is every one that continueth not in all things which are written in the book of the law to do them (Gal. 3:8-10).

Next, we investigated the development of the conflict over birth-right between Esau and Jacob and the birth of the twelve sons of Jacob. They became the progenitors of the twelve tribes of Israel. Then we saw that their descendants spent a short time in Israel, not up to 400 years, and were maltreated by a foreign ruler of Egypt from Assyria: *"For thus saith the Lord GOD, My people went down aforetime into Egypt to sojourn there; and the Assyrian oppressed them without cause"* (Is. 52:4). God then raised Moses to lead them into the "Promised Land," but all the adults that came out of Egypt died in the wilderness due to their unbelief. We demonstrated that via its esoteric meanings, these scriptures about Israel were just a foreshadowing of the real Israel, which was to come, namely those persons who come to understand and put their faith in Christ. We pointed out that just as those who had been "saved" from Egypt did not enter the promised land, so we were saved from separation from God could also end up not entering the Kingdom.

We looked at the period when Judges such as Samuel and Barak guided Israel (before they had a King). We likened it to the church/assembly without the Holy Ghost as a guide. We saw the coronation of the first King of Israel, Saul, and the character flaws that made God remove his dynasty. We saw the significance of the number three and how it related to the end of the corporate nation of Israel after the third King, Solomon. We saw how due to the rebellious character of the subsequent Kings in the divided kingdoms of Israel and Judah, God allowed other nations to put the peoples and their rulers into captivity until the time of Jesus Christ.

We then studied the ministry of Jesus, and the work of the Holy Ghost after him, a task that continues even today through the Holy Ghost and his Body. We looked at some characteristics of behavior that are displeasing to the Holy Ghost and showed that no sin could separate a believer from Christ except a "sin against the Holy Ghost." A sin against the Holy Ghost is simply persuading oneself that Christ is not who he says that he is, after once believing that he is.

Finally, we began to describe the second and third stages of existence in God for the natural universe. We described the second stage as the "coming of the son of man." This second stage is the period in which the Elect of God shall rule this universe for a *spiritual*

1000 years. We usually refer to this event is as the "Coming of the Lord." We went on to describe the third stage of Existence, which shall come after that, often referred to as the "New Heaven and New Earth." We said it was not too clear how to describe what existence would be like in these coming two epochs, but that we can see the next one more clearly than the latter. Simply put, the Tabernacle and the Temple had three Courts. So also does existence have three epochs. The first is the one we are in now. The second is the one often referred to as "the coming of the Lord," and the third comes after the "Great White Throne of Judgment:"

And I saw a great white throne, and him that sat on it, from whose face the earth and the heaven fled away; and there was found no place for them. And I saw the dead, small and great, stand before God; and the books were opened: and another book was opened, which is the book of life: and the dead were judged out of those things which were written in the books, according to their works. And the sea gave up the dead which were in it; and death and hell delivered up the dead which were in them: and they were judged every man according to their works. And death and hell were cast into the lake of fire. This is the second death. And whosoever was not found written in the book of life was cast into the lake of fire (Rev. 20:11-15).

And I saw a new heaven and a new earth: for the first heaven and the first earth were passed away; and there was no more sea. And I John saw the holy city, new Jerusalem, coming down from God out of heaven, prepared as a bride adorned for her husband. And I heard a great voice out of heaven saying, Behold, the tabernacle of God is with men, and he will dwell with them, and they shall be his people, and God himself shall be with them, and be their God. And God shall wipe away all tears from their eyes; and there shall be no more death, neither sorrow, nor crying, neither shall there be any more pain: for the former things are passed away. And he that sat upon the throne said, Behold, I make all things new. And he said unto me, Write: for these words are true and faithful (Rev. 21:1-5).

During the Reign of the Son of Man, an elect group transformed psychologically and Physiologically will have dominion over every nation. There will still be nations as we understand them today, but with some changes. Many countries that were possessed by force from the natural inhabitants will have to work out a new arrangement with the surviving descendants of the original inhabitants. *"And hath made of one blood all nations of men for to dwell on all the face of the earth, and hath determined the times before appointed, and the bounds of their habitation"* (Act. 17:26). This re-districting is because only the express command of God can violate the natural boundaries of people. It will certainly be a peaceful transition, not something done for revenge, but correction and atonement.

During the 1000-year reign of Christ, people will still be marrying and bearing children. The beautiful thing is that most marriages will be more in tune with the Will of God, and phenomena like divorce and spousal abuse will be nonexistent. Men and Women will have a different kind of marital relationship in which they will be equals in decision making, with each understanding both their strengths and weaknesses, working together to bring to pass the Will of God in their marriages. *"There is neither Jew nor Greek, there is neither bond nor free, there is neither male nor female: for ye are all one in Christ Jesus"* (Gal. 3:28). Of course, the Elect rulers will be a sort of Priestly Class and will not be marrying or given in marriage.

There will be little hunger, if any. The economy of the world will function in such a way as to have economic growth because people would be productively doing those things for which they are most suited. There will be a reduction to a minimum of stealing and other financial crimes, and anyone participating in such acts would be considered very unusual. This reduction is because the basic needs of all peoples would be met due to the Just rule of the elect, guided by the spirit of Christ in whom they permanently reside. *"And the king made silver and gold at Jerusalem as plenteous as stones, and cedar trees made he as the sycomore trees that are in the vale for abundance "*(2 Chron. 1:15).

As a reminder, I am NOT describing the "New Heaven and New Earth" but rather the millennial reign of Christ through the Sons of God. The "New Heaven and New Earth" happens AFTER the "Great White Throne of Judgement." The "Coming of The Lord" occurs when *"judgment was given to them."* You can refer to the period we live in now as the "sixth day," the 1000 years as the "seventh day," and the "New Heaven, New Earth" period as the "Eighth Day." In Genesis, we see that the Beasts were on earth before man on the sixth day. Just as we see in Daniel, chapter seven:

> *Thus he said, The fourth beast shall be the fourth kingdom upon earth, which shall be diverse from all kingdoms, and shall devour the whole earth, and shall tread it down, and break it in pieces. And the ten horns out of this kingdom are ten kings that shall arise: and another shall rise after them; and he shall be diverse from the first, and he shall subdue three kings. And he shall speak great words against the most High, and shall wear out the saints of the most High, and think to change times and laws: and they shall be given into his hand until a time and times and the dividing of time (7:23-25).*

The account of creation has both an esoteric and exoteric meaning. Just as the book of Daniel talks about the "Beasts," we can also see a spiritual correlation between Daniel's Beasts and the Beasts in Genesis. On one level, Genesis is referring to natural animals that we see. On another level, it was a prophecy that the beasts would rule the evening before the Son of Man would rule the Morning. Hence, the evening always comes first in Genesis One.

The main purpose of trying to describe the 1000 years is not to give an absolute description of exactly how things will be at that time but to show what the Bible indicates about that time to come, and that which is to occur after it. It is only the Elect that would have participated in the physiological change that gives them eternal life. The rest of humanity will have an opportunity to live in a world where there is a righteous rule and will be able to see the difference between the rule of Christ and the rule of men. Sadly, according to the bible, when God releases Satan for a period, he will be able to convince some people to rebel against the Elect. This rebellion will fail, but it will be evidence that there is something fundamentally wrong with man because of Sin. Only faith in Christ can redeem us from it:

> *And when the thousand years are expired, Satan shall be loosed out of his prison, And shall go out to deceive the nations which are in the four quarters of the earth, Gog and Magog, to gather them together to battle: the number of whom is as the sand of the sea. And they went up on the breadth of the earth, and compassed the camp of the saints about, and the beloved city: and fire came down from God out of heaven and devoured them* (Rev. 20:7-9).

As mentioned in several passages of scripture, the period before the 1000-year reign will be a time of economic and political turmoil. Such as we are experiencing in the early 21st century. The Signature character of the era is the personality referred to as "the Anti-Christ." We believe that this personality might not be a physical person, but the force of Modernity already calcifying and dissipating human morality:

> *Let no man deceive you by any means: for that day shall not come, except there come a falling away first, and that man of sin be revealed, the son of perdition; Who opposeth and exalteth himself above all that is called God, or that is worshipped;* **so that he as God sitteth in the temple of God, shewing himself that he is God**. *Remember ye not, that, when I was yet with you, I told you these things? And now ye know what withholdeth that he might be revealed in his time. For the mystery of iniquity doth already work: only he who now letteth will let, until he be taken out of the way. And then*

shall that Wicked be revealed, whom the Lord shall consume with the spirit of his mouth, and shall destroy with the brightness of his coming: Even him, whose coming is after the working of Satan with all power and signs and lying wonders, And with all deceivableness of unrighteousness in them that perish; because they received not the love of the truth, that they might be saved (2 Thess. 2:3-10).

When most people read this scripture, they think about a literal man. However, the very fact that this scripture states that "he sitteth in the temple," is an indication that this "man of sin" is unlikely a human being, because the Temple of God is the people of God and other human beings. Only a spirit can inhabit the people of God and other humans.

How has this spirit of Anti-Christ shown himself to be at work? By the values that are being forced upon the world today. For example, praying in Public institutions in certain "civilized" countries is now illegal. School children are no longer receiving religious education, on the pretext that it would "offend" others of a different faith. Most people forget that when the government introduced public schooling to parents, it was declared to be a place where teachers instill the values of the parents on a formal basis within institutions that were answerable to the parents. We have forgotten all that now. Public schools now teach the ideology of the anti-Christ to children.

This power of the "Beast" has also upturned the role of men and women. Today infants are born and then separated from their "working mothers" no later than a few weeks after they are born. The loving, nurturing period of a human child that used to last two to five years is now lost most of the current generation. The resultant effect has been a hardening of the soul and conscience of the children. The children of today are the most unemphatic people alive. However, this group is the generation that will be used by God to destroy the power of the Anti-Christ.

The relationship between the governed and the governments is one of distrust and clandestine surveillance. The government monitors every telephone call, email, text message, and entertainment channel. It is often justified in the name of national defense against terrorism, but every soul knows that something darker is at play. They even watch the watchers themselves. No one dares speak outside of the permitted group speak. Classes of people have been turned against each other by vain phenomena such as skin tone, national origin, or religious belief. We make women feel that their sex is a kind of disability that needs protection. The beauty and elegance that God intended for women to demonstrate through their reserved and humble nature are considered an expression of servitude. Yet, women were never less happy than they are now with this new phenomenon of "modernity" sweeping the world, leaving nothing but the destruction of culture and values in its wake.

These dissensions and economic troubles have led to endless wars, without defined and achievable objectives. These are a prelude to the ultimate war of Armageddon (not to be confused with the war of Gog and Magog, which comes later):

> *And he gathered them together into a place called in the Hebrew tongue Armageddon. And the seventh angel poured out his vial into the air; and there came a great voice out of the temple of heaven, from the throne, saying, It is done. And there were voices, and thunders, and lightnings; and there was a great earthquake, such as was not since men were upon the earth, so mighty an earthquake, and so great. And the great city was divided into three parts, and the cities of the nations fell: and great Babylon came in remembrance before God, to give unto her the cup of the wine of the fierceness of his wrath. And every island fled away, and the mountains were not found. And there fell upon men a great hail out of heaven, every stone about the weight of a talent: and men blasphemed God because of the plague of the hail; for the plague thereof was exceeding great* (Rev. 16:16-21).

All these physical manifestations of wars are simply a parallel to what is taking place simultaneously on a spiritual plane between the Elect and the Satanic forces.

The spiritual battle taking place now is for the control of a realm in each human being, referred to as "the Air." "*And you hath he quickened, who were dead in trespasses and sins; Wherein in time past ye walked according to the course of this world, according to the prince of the power of the air, the spirit that now worketh in the children of disobedience:*" (Eph. 2:1-2). This place in mankind is the point from which comes all the motivation for Good or Evil. Satan is in control of that realm, but some The Elect are wrestling for control of it with him. In the book of Revelation, in Chapter 12, where we read that there was war in "Heaven." This heaven is the same place referred to as "The Air" in Ephesians:

> *And there was war in heaven: Michael and his angels fought against the dragon; and the dragon fought and his angels, And prevailed not; neither was their place found any more in heaven. And the great dragon was cast out, that old serpent, called the Devil, and Satan, which deceiveth the whole world: he was cast out into the earth, and his angels were cast out with him. And I heard a loud voice saying in heaven, Now is come salvation, and strength, and the kingdom of our God, and the power of his Christ: for the accuser of our brethren is cast down, which accused them before our God day and night. And they*

overcame him by the blood of the Lamb, and by the word of their testimony; and they loved not their lives unto the death (Rev. 12:7-11).

Notice Michael's "angels" overcame Satan and his angels by the blood of Jesus and the Word of their testimony. The "angels" are Christians who are fighting in the spirit via truth and prayer. Furthermore, we read in 1 Thessalonians chapter 4 that we "shall meet the Lord in the Air" AFTER he DESCENDS FROM HEAVEN TO THE AIR. This meeting is significant. The spiritual battle taking place INSIDE of mankind is what is manifesting in this physical world as a troubled socio/economic and political problem.

After the Elect are "caught up," they will be able to cast down the powers that influence the souls of men toward the negative habits. The elect will accomplish this by taking control of the heavenly realm called "the air," where Satanic forces currently rule the earth. On the physical plane, a change would have also occurred in their physical bodies as it happened with Jesus after he rose from the dead. It is important to remember that, even though Jesus had a supernatural body when he rose from the dead, he had not yet received a spiritually glorified body. Nevertheless, he was able to walk through walls and appear and disappear at will:

And he said unto them, Why are ye troubled? and why do thoughts arise in your hearts? Behold my hands and my feet, that it is I myself: handle me, and see; for a spirit hath not flesh and bones, as ye see me have (Lk. 24:38-39).

As mentioned earlier, the number Three is God's number for completion. Therefore, to understand the doctrine of the resurrection, we must recognize the three-stage change of our physiological being. The first is taking place now as our "nature" sometimes called "flesh" is being transformed by the Holy Ghost "But *we all, with open face beholding as in a glass the glory of the Lord, are changed into the same image from glory to glory, even as by the Spirit of the Lord*" (2 Cor. 3:18). The second will occur at the "sound of the last trumpet" when we shall be changed in the twinkling of an eye "*In a moment, in the twinkling of an eye, at the last trump, for the trumpet shall sound, and the dead shall be raised incorruptible, and we shall be changed*" (1 Cor. 15:52). The third and final change, the GLORIFICATION OF OUR BODIES, will occur when the Heavenly Jerusalem "descends from God, Out of Heaven" after the Judgment:

And I saw a new heaven and a new earth: for the first heaven and the first earth were passed away; and there was no more sea. And I John saw the holy city, new Jerusalem, coming down from God out of heaven, prepared as a bride adorned for her husband.

And I heard a great voice out of heaven saying, Behold, the tabernacle of God is with men, and he will dwell with them, and they shall be his people, and God himself shall be with them, and be their God (Rev. 21:1-3).

The whole purpose of being a believer in Christ is to attain this final stage of change. We believe that these three stages are concomitant with the three stages of progression by the High Priests from the Outer Court, through the Holy Place, and eventually, into the Holy of Holies. As at now, only Jesus has been able to enter the third stage of change, but for those who obey and believe, we also shall be able to attain unto the "outer resurrection." "*That I may know him, and the power of his resurrection, and the fellowship of his sufferings, being made conformable unto his death; If by any means I might attain unto **the resurrection of the dead***" (Phil. 3:110-1). This event is a different resurrection from that which has been freely obtained for us by Jesus Christ. The Greek language used by the Holy Ghost here is "*Ek-Anastasis*," which means the "Out Resurrection." It is distinct from the general Resurrection "anastasis." Revelation refers to it as the "First Resurrection." It is not first in chronology, but simply superior in quality. It is only available to the Elect who "Overcome":

> *But the rest of the dead lived not again until the thousand years were finished. This is the first resurrection. Blessed and holy is he that hath part in the first resurrection: on such the second death hath no power, but they shall be priests of God and of Christ, and shall reign with him a thousand years* (Rev. 20:5-6).

In conclusion, we know that by Faith, God created the universe, and we are the crown jewel of his creation. We are going through the process of being completed even now. The finished product is a person that resembles and thinks like Jesus Christ. We are not there yet, but he is working on us by his spirit. The final product will be a new man in which God will dwell permanently. This man will be a man of Righteousness, Peace, and Joy in the Holy Ghost. This man will be The Kingdom of God on Earth:

For none of us liveth to himself, and no man dieth to himself. For whether we live, we live unto the Lord; and whether we die, we die unto the Lord: whether we live therefore, or die, we are the Lord's (Rom. 14:7-8).

Amen!

BIBLIOGRAPHY

Darwin, Charles. The Origin of Species by Means of Natural Selection, or the Preservation of Favored Races in the Struggle for Life. (John Murray,1859)

Ducille, Cecil J. The Book of Revelation: Vols. 1,2,3. (Sonlight Gospel Publishing, 1998).

Ducille, Cecil J. The Pattern. (Maranatha Press, 1995)

Gibson, Dan. Early Islamic Qiblas: A Survey of Mosques Built Between 622 CE & 876 CE. (Independent Scholars Press 2017)

Gibson, Dan. The Nabataeans: Builders of Petra. (Independent Scholars Press,2004)

Neusner, Jacob. A life of Yohanan Ben Zakkai 1 CE – 80 CE. (E.J. Brill 1970)

Päs, Heinrich. The Perfect Wave with Neutrinos at the Boundary of Space and Time. (Harvard University Press, 2014).

The Authorized King James Bible: Containing the Old and New Testaments. (Original work published 1611).

Vanamali, Devi. The Completer Life of Krishna Based on The Earliest Oral Traditions and The Sacred Scriptures. (Inner Traditions/Bear & Co. 2012)

Winters, Clyde J. Before Egypt: The Maa Confederation, Africa's First Civilization, (Uthman Dan Fodio Institute, 2013).

Printed in the United States
By Bookmasters